"Knowing is not enough; we must apply.
Willing is not enough; we must do."
—Goethe

INSTITUTE OF MEDICINE

Shaping the Future for Health

THE NATIONAL ACADEMIES

National Academy of Sciences
National Academy of Engineering
Institute of Medicine
National Research Council

The **National Academy of Sciences** is a private, nonprofit, self-perpetuating society of distinguished scholars engaged in scientific and engineering research, dedicated to the furtherance of science and technology and to their use for the general welfare. Upon the authority of the charter granted to it by the Congress in 1863, the Academy has a mandate that requires it to advise the federal government on scientific and technical matters. Dr. Bruce M. Alberts is president of the National Academy of Sciences.

The **National Academy of Engineering** was established in 1964, under the charter of the National Academy of Sciences, as a parallel organization of outstanding engineers. It is autonomous in its administration and in the selection of its members, sharing with the National Academy of Sciences the responsibility for advising the federal government. The National Academy of Engineering also sponsors engineering programs aimed at meeting national needs, encourages education and research, and recognizes the superior achievements of engineers. Dr. Wm. A. Wulf is president of the National Academy of Engineering.

The **Institute of Medicine** was established in 1970 by the National Academy of Sciences to secure the services of eminent members of appropriate professions in the examination of policy matters pertaining to the health of the public. The Institute acts under the responsibility given to the National Academy of Sciences by its congressional charter to be an adviser to the federal government and, upon its own initiative, to identify issues of medical care, research, and education. Dr. Kenneth I. Shine is president of the Institute of Medicine.

The **National Research Council** was organized by the National Academy of Sciences in 1916 to associate the broad community of science and technology with the Academy's purposes of furthering knowledge and advising the federal government. Functioning in accordance with general policies determined by the Academy, the Council has become the principal operating agency of both the National Academy of Sciences and the National Academy of Engineering in providing services to the government, the public, and the scientific and engineering communities. The Council is administered jointly by both Academies and the Institute of Medicine. Dr. Bruce M. Alberts and Dr. Wm. A. Wulf are chairman and vice chairman, respectively, of the National Research Council.

Coverage Matters

Insurance and Health Care

Committee on the Consequences of Uninsurance

Board on Health Care Services

INSTITUTE OF MEDICINE

NATIONAL ACADEMY PRESS
Washington, D.C.

8762643

NATIONAL ACADEMY PRESS • 2101 Constitution Avenue, N.W. • Washington, DC 20418

NOTICE: The project that is the subject of this report was approved by the Governing Board of the National Research Council, whose members are drawn from the councils of the National Academy of Sciences, the National Academy of Engineering, and the Institute of Medicine. The members of the committee responsible for the report were chosen for their special competences and with regard for appropriate balance.

Support for this project was provided by The Robert Wood Johnson Foundation. The views presented in this report are those of the Institute of Medicine Committee on the Consequences of Uninsurance and are not necessarily those of the funding agencies.

International Standard Book Number 0-309-07609-9

Additional copies of this report are available for sale from the National Academy Press, 2101 Constitution Avenue, N.W., Box 285, Washington, D.C. 20055. Call (800) 624-6242 or (202) 334-3313 (in the Washington metropolitan area), or visit the NAP's home page at **www.nap.edu.** The full text of this report is available at **www.nap.edu.**

For more information about the Institute of Medicine, visit the IOM home page at **www.iom.edu.**

The serpent has been a symbol of long life, healing, and knowledge among almost all cultures and religions since the beginning of recorded history. The serpent adopted as a logotype by the Institute of Medicine is a relief carving from ancient Greece, now held by the Staatliche Museen in Berlin.

COMMITTEE ON THE CONSEQUENCES OF UNINSURANCE

IOM Staff

Wilhelmine Miller, Project Co-director
Dianne Miller Wolman, Project Co-director
Lynne Page Snyder, Program Officer
Tracy McKay, Research Assistant
Ryan Palugod, Project Assistant

Reviewers

This report has been reviewed in draft form by individuals chosen for their diverse perspectives and technical expertise, in accordance with procedures approved by the NRC's Report Review Committee. The purpose of this independent review is to provide candid and critical comments that will assist the institution in making its published report as sound as possible and to ensure that the report meets institutional standards for objectivity, evidence, and responsiveness to the study charge. The review comments and draft manuscript remain confidential to protect the integrity of the deliberative process. We wish to thank the following individuals for their review of this report:

BRUCE BRADLEY, Director, Managed Care Plans, General Motors Health Care Initiatives, Detroit, Michigan

HARRY P. CAIN, Adjunct Faculty Member, Graduate School of Business, College of William and Mary, Williamsburg, Virginia

JACOB FELDMAN, Senior Fellow, Center for Health Affairs, Project HOPE, Bethesda, Maryland

ROBERT L. JOHNSON, Professor of Pediatrics & Clinical Psychiatry, Director, Adolescent & Young Adult Medicine, University of Medicine and Dentistry of New Jersey, New Jersey Medical School, Newark

SCOTT C. RATZAN, Senior Technical Advisor and Population Leadership Fellow, Center for Population, Health, and Nutrition, U.S. Agency for International Development, Washington, D.C.

DIANE ROWLAND, Executive Vice President, Henry J. Kaiser Family Foundation, Executive Director, The Kaiser Commission on Medicaid and the Uninsured, Washington, D.C.

FRANK A. SLOAN, J. Alexander McMahon Professor of Health Policy and Management, Professor of Economics, Director, Center for Health Policy, Law & Management, Duke University, Durham, North Carolina

KATHERINE SWARTZ, Professor of Health Economics, Department of Health Policy and Management, Harvard School of Public Health, Boston, Massachusetts

DAVID TAKEUCHI, Professor of Sociology, Indiana University, Bloomington

Although the reviewers listed above have provided many constructive comments and suggestions, they were not asked to endorse the conclusions or recommendations nor did they see the final draft of the report before its release. The review of this report was overseen by **Hugh H. Tilson, Adjunct Professor, School of Public Health, University of North Carolina, Chapel Hill**, appointed by the Institute of Medicine and **Joseph P. Newhouse, John D. MacArthur Professor of Health Policy & Management, Harvard University**, appointed by the NRC's Report Review Committee, who were responsible for making certain that an independent examination of this report was carried out in accordance with institutional procedures and that all review comments were carefully considered. Responsibility for the final content of this report rests entirely with the authoring committee and the institution.

Preface

This is the first report in a series of six that the Institute of Medicine (IOM) Committee on the Consequences of Uninsurance will issue over the next two years to evaluate and consolidate our knowledge of the causes and consequences of lacking health insurance. The Committee was established just one year ago with the charge of reviewing and assessing evidence across a spectrum of disciplines to expand our understanding of the problem of uninsurance. The Committee agreed to undertake this formidable task in order to delineate more clearly the personal, family, community, and economic consequences of the existing public and private health insurance mechanisms—a system that leaves almost one out of six Americans without coverage.

This initial report of the Committee establishes both a conceptual framework and baseline data about the magnitude and extent of the problem nationwide. It seeks to answer the basic questions of who, when, where, and why so many Americans lack health insurance. The report provides an overview of health insurance in America, describes the dynamic and often unstable nature of insurance coverage, profiles populations that frequently lack coverage, and identifies factors that make it more or less likely that a person will be uninsured at some point in life. Finally, the report outlines the research agenda that the Committee will pursue in this series of six reports.

Many people have made substantial contributions to this report. The Subcommittee on the Status of the Uninsured, chaired by Willard Manning, produced a draft for the full Committee's consideration within an extraordinarily short time and continued to work with the full Committee in revising the initial draft. Committee members John Ayanian, Sheila Davis, Willard Manning, and Larry Wallack were joined on the subcommittee by Peter Cunningham, Paul Fronstin, and Catherine Hoffman, who generously contributed their expertise to the report throughout its conceptualization and drafting. Committee member Ron Andersen advised the subcommittee from the start as it devised the conceptual framework that will be employed throughout the series of studies. IOM staff under Study Co-directors Dianne Wolman and Wilhelmine Miller provided excellent research and writing support to the subcommittee and Committee throughout their delibera-tions. Program Officer Lynne Snyder served as lead staff analyst on this report.

We hope that this report will stimulate public dialogue and a reexamina-tion of long-standing issues of health care financing and continuity of coverage. The Committee's future reports on health outcomes for the uninsured, family impacts of lacking health insurance, implications for communities, the economic costs to society as a whole, and models of reform will provide in-depth and closely considered information that should sustain and hopefully advance policy debates about health care coverage. We are grateful to The Robert Wood Johnson Foun-dation for its support of the Committee's work.

Mary Sue Coleman, Ph.D.
Co-chair
Arthur Kellermann, M.D., M.P.H.
Co-chair
September 2001

Foreword

Coverage Matters: Insurance and Health Care is the first installment of a sustained effort by the Institute of Medicine (IOM) to inform the debate about a pressing and persistent challenge to American health care and public policy: lack of health insurance for about 40 million Americans. In 1999, the IOM determined that this long-standing problem should be a priority of the Institute's policy research agenda. We are grateful to The Robert Wood Johnson Foundation for support of a series of six studies addressing the personal and social impacts of uninsurance. This is the first report in that series. The 16-member IOM Committee on the Consequences of Uninsurance brings an exceptional breadth of experience to this project. Its members have backgrounds in clinical medicine, epidemiology, public health, nursing, health services organization, health and labor economics, strategic corporate planning and small businesses, academic health care, and provision of care to those without coverage and other populations at risk.

This first report of the Committee lays the groundwork for subsequent reports that will identify the costs and consequences for individuals, families, communities, and American society when a large population of individuals does not have health insurance. Although much of the information in this initial report has been available before, *Coverage Matters* integrates findings from an extensive public policy, economics, and health services research literature to produce a coherent and comprehensible account of who has and who lacks health insurance, and why. This report provides the reader with a road map to subsequent reports, outlining both their content and the analytical framework that the Committee will employ to look at a wide range of impacts. The second report, which will follow in about nine months, will examine the evidence accumulated to date about the risks and health consequences of lacking health insurance, both sporadically and, especially, for extended periods of time. Policy makers and general readers alike should find this initial report and the five to follow a valuable contribution to their understanding of a matter of vital concern to us all—the consequences of having millions of uninsured Americans.

Kenneth I. Shine, M.D.
President, Institute of Medicine
September 2001

Acknowledgments

A project of this scale and complexity requires a team effort. Many individuals have contributed to the quality of this first report. The Committee takes this opportunity to recognize several of those who have helped.

At the beginning of such an extensive effort, gathering information is crucial. Many health policy researchers and others contributed to a workshop in December 2000 and to public Committee sessions then and in April 2001. Gerry Fairbrother, Hanns Kuttner, Edward Maibach, and Jack Needleman, consultants to the Committee, prepared background papers and served on workshop panels. Other presenters at the workshop were E. Richard Brown, Thomas Buchmueller, Peter Cunningham, Darrell Gaskin, Jack Hadley, Karla Hanson, Catherine Hoffman, Judith Kasper, Genevieve Kenney, Ronda Kotelchuck, Nicole Lurie, Kristin Moore, Keith Mueller, Julie Rovner, Cathy Schoen, Lawrence Wallack, Ray Werntz, and Charlotte Yeh. William Hall, Catherine McLaughlin, Diane Rowland, Steven Schroeder, and Anne Weiss addressed the Committee during its public meetings.

This first report has benefited from the participation of consultants who provided guidance and technical expertise. Edward Maibach and Diana Rubin of Porter Novelli provided communications advice, and Hanns Kuttner and Eugene Moyer provided economic and statistical expertise. Anirban Basu contributed his time in the preparation of original data analyses presented in this report, and the Committee extends special thanks to him.

The Committee specifically acknowledges the members of the Subcommittee on the Status of the Uninsured, which developed this foundational first report: Willard Manning (chair), John Ayanian, Peter Cunningham, Sheila Davis, Paul Fronstin, Catherine Hoffman, and Larry Wallack.

The Committee recognizes the hard work of staff at the Institute of Medicine (IOM). This work is conducted under the guidance of Janet Corrigan, director, Board on Health Care Services, who planned and developed this project along with IOM leadership and the sponsor. The project team, directed by Wilhelmine Miller and Dianne Wolman, worked under a very tight schedule to produce this first report. Dianne managed the publication process and edited the report. Wilhelmine guided its substantive development. Program Officer Lynne Snyder was lead analyst and made sense out of an enormous body of information within a very short time. Research Assistant Tracy McKay served as sole support staff during the crucial startup period of the Committee and worked tirelessly and expertly to organize and prepare background materials for the December workshop. She also prepared the manuscript for publication. Project Assistant Ryan Palugod provided support in the development of databases, managed meeting logistics, and conducted Web research.

Funding for the project comes from The Robert Wood Johnson Foundation (RWJF). The committee extends special thanks to Steven Schroeder, president, and Anne Weiss, senior project officer, RWJF, for their support and thoughtful attention.

Finally, the Committee would like to thank the chairs, Mary Sue Coleman and Arthur Kellermann, for their leadership and dedication to the project. The chairs, in turn, thank the committee members for their commitment and contributions of time and expertise to this report and to those that follow.

Contents

Coverage
Matters

Executive Summary

Health care increasingly affects our personal lives and the national economy as its benefits to our health, longevity and quality of life grow. Over the past quarter of a century, clinical medicine has become more sophisticated, technological advances have become more commonplace, and the range of health care interventions has been much expanded. Yet over the same period, the numbers of persons without health insurance to help them purchase health services has increased by about one million per year—faster than the rate of overall population growth. The total number of uninsured Americans grew even during years of economic prosperity (Holahan and Kim, 2000).

This report and the five reports that will follow endeavor to present a wide-angle view of health insurance and examine the consequences of being without insurance, not only for persons who are uninsured and their families, but also for the communities in which they live and for society. Health insurance is one of the best-known and most common means used to obtain access to health care. What are the consequences for all of us of having tens of millions of people uninsured?

Over the next two years, the Institute of Medicine Committee on the Consequences of Uninsurance will evaluate and report what is known about the impacts of being uninsured and how being uninsured affects individuals, families, communities, and society. The Committee will focus on *un*insured people, defined as persons with no health insurance and no assistance in paying for health care beyond what is available through charity and safety-net institutions. It recognizes, however, that many people have insurance that offers incomplete coverage and that being *under*insured poses problems as well, though these are generally less severe. While the implications and potentially harmful consequences are greater for those who are uninsured for longer periods, in this report we consider persons who lack insurance for any period of time to be uninsured and at risk for some adverse effects as a result.

Many professional societies, private foundations, government agencies, and political and consumer organizations have highlighted detrimental health and financial impacts for individuals and families of being uninsured. Research and information about these impacts are extensive but widely scattered. By constituting and charging this Committee, the Institute of Medicine recognizes both the urgency of the issues surrounding health insurance coverage of the U.S. population and the need for consolidating and critically appraising evidence regarding the impacts of uninsurance for individuals and communities. In presenting its evaluation of the research literature and findings about the health and economic consequences of uninsurance, the Committee hopes to add context and depth to the ongoing public dialogue about these issues, by focusing on the connections between the lack of coverage and a variety of documented personal and social outcomes.

In this first report, the Committee provides an overview of health insurance in America, looking specifically at how coverage is gained and lost, why so many people have none, and who lacks insurance, as individuals and as members of groups within the general population. In addition, this report introduces the Committee's analytic plan for the entire series of reports and presents the conceptual framework that will guide the Committee's evaluations of specific impacts of uninsurance in its subsequent reports.

MYTHS AND REALITIES

This report begins by examining pervasive popular ideas about the scope and nature of the problem of uninsurance that frustrate attempts to address this complex issue constructively. Americans persistently underestimate the numbers of uninsured people and hold many misperceptions about their identity, about how one becomes uninsured, and about the economic and health consequences of being uninsured (Fronstin, 1998; Blendon et al., 1999; News-Hour–Kaiser, 2000; Wirthlin Worldwide, 2001).

Myth: People without health insurance get the medical care they need.

Reality: **The uninsured are much more likely than persons with insurance coverage to go without needed care** (Schoen and DesRoches, 2000). They also receive fewer preventive services and less regular care for chronic conditions than people with insurance (Ayanian et al., 2000; Baker et al., 2000).

Myth: The number of uninsured Americans is not particularly large and has not been increasing in recent years.

Reality: **The number of uninsured people is greater than the combined populations of Texas, Florida, and Connecticut. During 1999, the Census Bureau estimated that approximately 42 million people in the United States lacked health insurance coverage** (Mills, 2000). **This number represents about 15 percent of a total population of 274 million**

persons and 17 percent of the population under 65 years of age.[1] An estimated ten million of the uninsured are children under the age of 18 (about 14 percent of all children), and about 32 million are adults between ages 18 and 65 (about 19 percent of all adults in this group) (Mills, 2000). The estimate of uninsured people is even larger when coverage is measured over several years. **Almost three out of every ten Americans, more than 70 million people, lacked health insurance for at least a month over a 36-month period** (Bennefield, 1998a).

Estimates of the number of persons who lack insurance vary depending on the survey and range from 32 million to 42 million for those without coverage throughout the year.[2] Surveys differ in their size and sampling methods, the ways in which questions are asked about insurance coverage, and the period over which insurance coverage or uninsurance is measured (Lewis et al., 1998; Fronstin, 2000a). The Current Population Survey (CPS), conducted annually by the Census Bureau, is the most widely cited source of estimates of the number of uninsured persons and is used throughout this report as the primary data source. The CPS is particularly useful because it produces yearly estimates in a timely fashion, reporting the previous year's insurance coverage rates each September, and because information about insurance coverage has been gathered since the mid-1970s, allowing for analysis of coverage trends over time (Figure ES.1). Although the CPS nominally reports persons uninsured throughout the entire calendar year, some analysts believe that its estimates actually reflect shorter periods of uninsurance, and thus that its estimates of the number uninsured throughout the year are too high (Swartz, 1986).

Whether one uses the estimate of 42 million uninsured, as reported by the CPS, or the lower estimates generated on the basis of other governmentally and privately sponsored surveys, the number of uninsured Americans is substantial. In light of the CPS's usefulness and its limitations, this report relies on estimates based on CPS data, with caveats. The Committee finds the variation in estimates among surveys less critical than the order of magnitude of the entire range of estimates that different surveys yield.

Myth: Most people who lack health insurance are in families where no one works.

Reality: **More than 80 percent of uninsured children and adults under the age of 65 live in working families.** Although working does improve the chances that one and one's family will have insurance, even members of

---

[1]Because the federal Medicare program provides nearly universal coverage for persons at least 65 years of age, the Committee's work will focus on uninsured persons under age 65.

[2]For 1996, the Medical Expenditure Panel Survey (MEPS), conducted by the Agency for Healthcare Research and Quality, generated an estimate of 32 million nonelderly persons uninsured throughout the year. For the same year, the Census Bureau's CPS estimated 41 million uninsured defined the same way (Fronstin, 2000a).

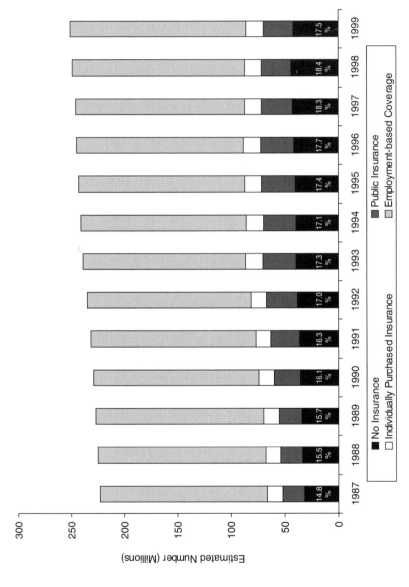

FIGURE ES.1 Sources of health insurance coverage for persons under age 65 years, 1987–1999.
SOURCE: Fronstin, 2000d.

families with two full-time wage earners have almost a one-in-ten chance of being uninsured (Hoffman and Pohl, 2000).

Myth: Growth in the numbers of recent immigrants has been a major source of the increase in the number of uninsured persons.

Reality: **Although immigrants who have arrived within 4 years have higher-than-average uninsurance rates, they comprise a relatively small proportion of the general population.** In fact, between 1994 and 1998, there has been a net decrease in the number of recently arrived immigrants (Holahan et al., 2001). Overall, noncitizens account for fewer than one in five uninsured persons (Mills, 2000).

Through its work, the Committee hopes to replace misperceptions with facts and in doing so, to lay the groundwork for a more informed public debate about health insurance coverage.

RELATING HEALTH INSURANCE TO ACCESS TO HEALTH SERVICES

Health insurance serves multiple constituencies and distinct purposes. For individuals and families, insurance coverage is one means to promote health and access to care and to protect against exceptional health care costs. Insurance pools the risks and resources of a group of people so that each is protected from financially disruptive medical expenses and each may plan ahead or budget for health care. In contrast with many other insurance products, such as automobile or homeowner's insurance, health insurance has evolved as a mechanism for financing routine health care expenses and encouraging the use of preventive services, in addition to protecting against uncommon events and expenses. As the scope and effectiveness of health care interventions have grown, so have consumers' expectations for coverage and benefits through health insurance.

Other constituencies also have a stake in our mechanisms for financing health care. Providers of health care benefit from insurance as a reliable source of payment. Employers offer health benefits to attract and retain workers and to maintain a productive workforce. Governments provide health insurance to special populations as a means to secure health care for them.

Health insurance is neither necessary nor sufficient to obtain health care, yet coverage remains one of the most important ways to obtain access to health services. The level of out-of-pocket costs for care has been demonstrated to have substantial effects on the use of health services (Newhouse et al., 1993; Zweifel and Manning, 2000). Uninsured persons may be charged more than patients with coverage, who benefit from discounts negotiated by their insurer (Wielawski, 2000; Kolata, 2001). In addition, uninsured people face 100 percent cost sharing, although some providers are willing to absorb part of the cost for some of their patients some of the time by negotiating a reduced rate. Even though many publicly supported institutions offer free care or reduced fees and many other providers offer some charity care, people without insurance generally have reduced access to care (Cunningham and Kemper 1998; Cunningham and Whitmore, 1998).

Evidence accumulated over the past several decades of health services research has consistently found that persons without insurance are less likely to have any physician visit within a year, have fewer visits annually, and are less likely to have a regular source of care (Andersen and Aday, 1978; Aday et al., 1984; Hafner-Eaton, 1993; Weissman and Epstein, 1994; Newacheck et al., 1998; Zweifel and Manning, 2000). Children without insurance are three times as likely as children with Medicaid coverage to have no regular source of care (15 percent of uninsured children do not have a regular provider compared with just 5 percent of children with Medicaid), and uninsured adults are more than three times as likely as either privately or publicly insured adults to lack a regular source of care (35 percent compared with 11 percent) (Haley and Zuckerman, 2000). The likelihood that those without health insurance lack a regular source of care has increased substantially since 1977 (Zuvekas and Weinick, 1999; Weinick et al., 2000).

Uninsured adults are less likely to receive health services, even for certain serious conditions. One nationally representative survey that took into account age, sex, income, and health status found that uninsured people were less than half as likely as those with insurance to receive needed care, as judged by physicians, for a serious medical condition (Baker et al., 2000). People without insurance are also less likely to receive preventive services and appropriate routine care for chronic conditions than those with insurance, even as the importance of preventive care and the prevalence of chronic disease become more prominent elements within health care (Hafner-Eaton, 1993; Burstin et al., 1998; Ayanian et al., 2000; Schoen and DesRoches, 2000; Institute of Medicine, 2001).

To guide its assessment of the relationship between the lack of health insurance, access to care, and the consequences of no coverage, the Committee has based its conceptual framework on a widely used behavioral model of access to health services (Figure ES.2) (Andersen, 1995; Andersen and Davidson, 2001). In this framework the major determinants of insurance coverage are heavily, but not exclusively, economic. The model links these determinants to features of the process of obtaining health services and to morbidity, mortality, and health status. Insurance coverage is thus linked in this model to an array of outcomes through the mediating effect of health care services. The model allows us to track the effects from lack of coverage on individuals and families, in a sizable uninsured population, to the viability of health care providers and institutions at a community level and the implications for the nation's economy.

HOW COVERAGE IS GAINED AND LOST

In the United States, health insurance is a voluntary matter, yet many people are involuntarily without coverage. There is no guarantee for most people under the age of 65 years that they will be eligible for, or able to afford to

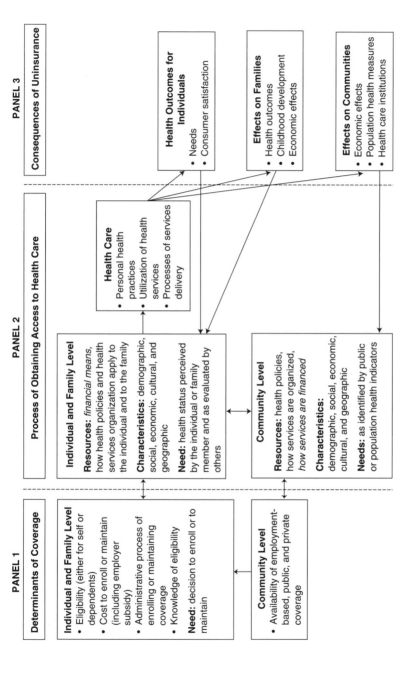

FIGURE ES.2 A conceptual framework for evaluating the consequences of uninsurance—a cascade of effects. NOTE: Italics indicate terms that include direct measures of health insurance coverage.

purchase or retain, health insurance. The historical tension rooted in American social values, between considering health care as a market commodity and as a social good, has fostered the development of variegated and complex arrangements for financing the delivery of health care (Stevens, 1989; Stone, 1993).

Within the private sector, insurance coverage depends on an employer's decision to offer a health benefit plan and an employee's decision to enroll or take up this offer (Figure ES.3). When workers are not offered the chance to purchase employment-based insurance for themselves and their dependent family members (spouses and minor children), or when they decline to enroll, individual policies and public insurance (Medicaid or the State Children's Health Insurance Program [SCHIP]) offer limited opportunities for coverage. Poor health status or low income may preclude the purchase of an affordable (or any) individual policy from an insurance company. The combination of strict eligibility requirements and complex enrollment procedures often makes public coverage difficult to obtain and even more difficult to maintain over time.

Opportunities to Purchase Coverage

Almost seven out of every ten Americans under age 65 years (66 percent) are covered by employment-based health insurance, from either their job or that of their parent or spouse (Fronstin, 2000d). Among workers 76 percent are offered health insurance by their employers, and 83 percent of those offered insurance decide to purchase or take up the offer of coverage (Fronstin, 2001). The 17 percent of workers that decline an employer's offer include about 13 percent who are covered through a spouse or elsewhere and 4 percent who remain uninsured. The expense and competing demands on family income are the main reasons given for declining the offer of employment-based insurance (Cooper and Schone, 1997; Rowland et al., 1998; Hoffman and Schlobohm, 2000).

Individually purchased policies and public insurance (primarily Medicaid) both fill some of the coverage gaps created by the employment-based system. Together they account for 21 percent of coverage.[3] Self-employed people (about 10 percent of workers) and their families must often rely on individually purchased health insurance. Individual coverage also serves as a stop-gap measure, however, for adult children who lose their coverage as dependents before they can obtain job-based coverage and for retirees under the age of 65 before they become eligible for Medicare. Medicaid coverage also tends to be transitory, with two-thirds of new enrollees losing coverage within the first year (Carrasquillo et al., 1998; Short and Freedman, 1998).

---

[3]Some people report multiple sources of coverage, so employment-based, individual, and public insurance coverage rates total more than the 82 percent of the U.S. population with any coverage during the year.

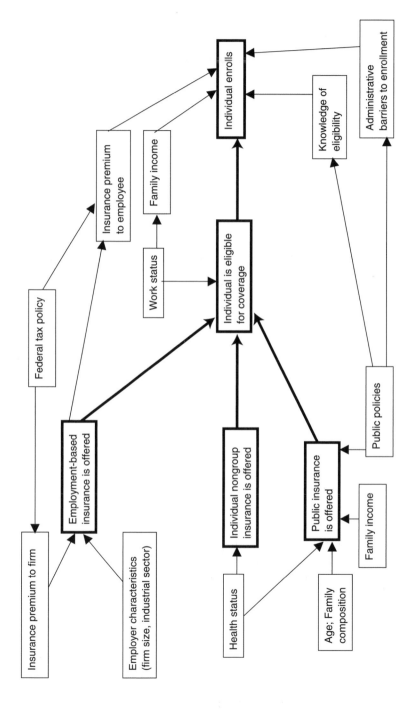

FIGURE ES.3 Factors affecting eligibility and enrollment.
NOTE: Bold lines indicate major pathways and decision points.

Gaining and Losing Coverage

Many normal social and economic transitions can trigger a loss of health insurance coverage for a person or family because income, health status, marital status, and terms of employment affect eligibility for and participation in health insurance. Conversely, many of these transitional events can result in becoming eligible for coverage. Because so many different common events are associated with a change in health insurance status, the chance of being uninsured over the course of a lifetime may be substantial. For example, a young adult (18–24) has a greater-than-even chance of being uninsured for at least one month over a 36-month period (Bennefield, 1998a).

For some people, lack of insurance is a temporary or one-time interruption of coverage, while for others, being uninsured is an experience that recurs periodically or may last for several years. Lower income persons tend to remain uninsured for longer than do those with incomes above the federal poverty level (McBride, 1997). Educational attainment and employment sector are factors that also are related to the length of uninsured periods (Swartz et al., 1993a). Short periods without health insurance are less likely than longer periods to adversely affect access to health services (Ayanian et al., 2000). Yet even short periods without insurance carry with them the financial risk of extraordinarily high health expenses.

Limited Coverage Options

Insurance industry underwriting practices, the costs of health services, and the patchwork of public policies regarding insurance coverage all contribute to the economic pressures on employers, insurers, and government programs offering health insurance. Small employers frequently face higher group health insurance premium rates than large employers do. Larger firms can cushion themselves from the financial impact of insurance company medical underwriting and restrictions by choosing to self-insure their employees' health benefits. Small employers may receive poorer benefits for premiums comparable to those of large firms, because of both a higher risk premium and higher administrative costs per person, and inadequate resources to evaluate and negotiate good coverage. As a result, some small employers may decline to offer coverage altogether. Among a group of 955 small businesses (fewer than 50 employees) surveyed, the most common and the highest-ranking reason for not offering insurance benefits was the expense of coverage (Fronstin and Helman, 2000).

The expense and competing demands on family income are the main reasons given by individuals for declining an offer of employment-based coverage. Wage-earners who accept or take up an employer's offer of a subsidized health benefit typically pay between one-quarter and one-third of the total cost of their insurance premium, in addition to deductibles, copayments, and the costs of health services that are not covered or are covered only in part. For families earning less than 200 percent of the federal poverty level (FPL), $33,400 for a family of four in 1999, the cost of an unsubsidized insurance premium may exceed 10 percent of annual income (Gabel et al., 1998).

Coverage Trends over Time

Since the mid-1970s, growth in the cost of health insurance has outpaced the rise in real income, creating a gap in purchasing ability that has added roughly one million persons to the ranks of the uninsured each year. These cost increases result in part from advances in medical and pharmaceutical technology, an aging population, and reduced consumer sensitivity to prices through expanded insurance coverage (Heffler et al., 2001). Despite the economic prosperity of recent years, between 1998 and 1999 there was only a slight drop in the number and proportion of uninsured Americans. Through the early 1990s the rising uninsurance rate reflected a decline in employment-based coverage. Since the mid-1990s increases in employment-based coverage have been offset by steady or declining rates of public and individually purchased coverage (Fronstin, 2000d).

A PORTRAIT OF THE UNINSURED

People lack coverage regardless of education, age, or state of residence. Employment and geographic factors are central because private insurance is closely tied to employment, and eligibility for public programs is partly determined by work and income criteria.

Social and Economic Factors Affect Coverage

Full-time, full-year employment offers families the best chance of having health insurance, as does an annual income of at least a moderate level (greater than 200 percent of FPL) (Custer and Ketsche, 2000b). Wage earners in smaller firms, lower-waged firms, nonunionized firms, and nonmanufacturing employment sectors are more likely than average to go without coverage. Members of families without wage earners are more likely to be uninsured than are members of families with wage earners. Two-thirds of all uninsured persons are members of lower-income families (earning less than 200 percent of FPL), and nearly one-third of all members of lower-income families are uninsured. More than one-quarter of all uninsured adults have not earned a high school diploma, and almost four out of every ten adults who have not graduated from high school are uninsured.

Coverage Varies over the Life Cycle

The average individual's chances of being uninsured trace a curve across the life span, from a lower-than-average likelihood for minor children and a higher-than-average likelihood for young adults to a gradual decline in probability with advancing age and increasing connection to the labor force. People 65 and older have a minimal likelihood of being uninsured because Medicare provides virtually universal coverage to that age group. Marriage and the rearing of infants and young children both decrease the chances, on average, that an adult will be uninsured. Sources of coverage and health status, as well as participation in the work force, also affect one's chances of lacking coverage.

Demographic Disparities in Coverage

Higher uninsured rates among members of racial and ethnic minority groups and among recent immigrants reflect their lower rates of employment-based coverage and lower family incomes, on average, compared to non-Hispanic whites and U.S.-born residents. African Americans are twice as likely as non-Hispanic whites to be uninsured, and Hispanics are three times as likely to be uninsured, although more than half of all uninsured persons are non-Hispanic whites. Foreign-born residents are almost three times as likely to be uninsured as are those born in the United States, and among the foreign born, noncitizens are more than twice as likely as citizens to be uninsured (Mills, 2000).

In addition, there are gender disparities in coverage, reflecting the different experiences of adult men and women in the workplace and with public policies. Although men are more likely than women to be uninsured, women have a lower rate of employment-based coverage. Because women are more likely to obtain coverage through individual policies and public programs, their insurance status tends to be less stable, with more opportunities for gaps in coverage (Miles and Parker, 1997; Fronstin, 2000b).

Geographic Differences Affect Coverage

The decentralized labor and health services markets of the United States and the distinctive public policies of each state and locality together create unique contexts for the patterns of insurance coverage for individuals, families, and population groups. Differences among the states with respect to population characteristics, industrial economic base, eligibility for public insurance, and relative purchasing power of family income shape the geographic disparities in insurance coverage rates (Figure ES.4) (Marsteller et al., 1998; Brown et al., 2000b; Cunningham and Ginsburg, 2001). Residents of the South and West are more likely than average to be uninsured. Reflecting the predominantly urban location of the general population, most uninsured persons live in urban areas, although rural and urban residents are about equally likely to be uninsured.

Factors Influencing Uninsured Rates

The Committee conducted a multivariate statistical analysis to estimate the

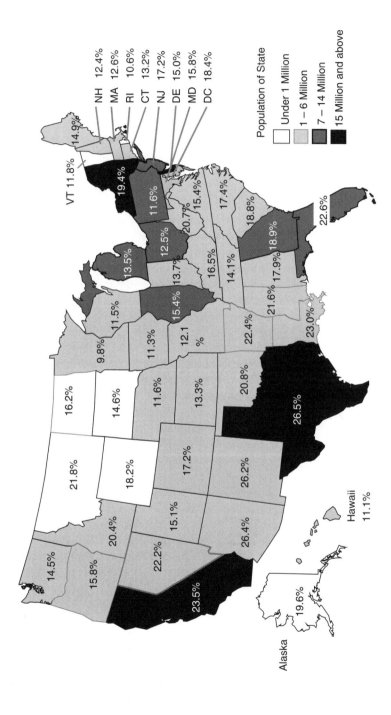

FIGURE ES.4 Probability of persons under age 65 being uninsured, by state, 1997–1999.
SOURCE: Hoffman and Pohl, 2000.

relative influence of a number of measured socioeconomic, demographic, and geographic characteristics. Bivariate analyses are also reported for these characteristics. According to this multivariate analysis, the variation in estimated uninsured rates among population groups diminishes substantially when income, occupation, employment sector and firm size, education, health status, age, gender, race and ethnicity, citizenship, and geography are included. This more elaborate statistical analysis confirms the qualitative impact found by simpler analyses of rates of uninsurance along single dimensions. It also supports the finding that employment-related factors, such as income, education, and economic sector, underlie much of the variation in uninsured rates among different population groups.

ANALYTIC PLAN FOR THE COMMITTEE

In future reports the Committee will look at an array of consequences of uninsurance and address its distinctive effects on successively larger and more complex entities. The conceptual framework developed in this report will guide the analyses in each of the subsequent reports, which will include examinations of health outcomes, financial impacts, and changes in the quality of life that result from the lack of health insurance.

Report 2: Health Consequences for Individuals

We know that insurance coverage facilitates access to health services, but what effects does the lack of health insurance have on health? In its second report the Committee will assess published evidence about how being uninsured affects many aspects of health for adults, including overall health status, disease-specific morbidity, avoidable hospitalizations, and mortality.

Report 3: Health and Economic Consequences for Families

When even one member of a family goes without health insurance, what consequences are shared by the entire family? Because children depend on their parents or other adults to obtain health care for them, their parents' experiences with the health care system, beliefs about health care, financial resources, and ability to negotiate that system on their children's behalf are important for childrens' health care. Each of these elements is affected, in turn, by a parent's or child's lack of insurance coverage. In its third report the Committee will assess the evidence about how family patterns of health insurance coverage affect both children's health and well-being and families' economic stability and security.

Report 4: Consequences for Communities

What are the health and economic consequences for communities of having large uninsured populations? In its fourth report the Committee will consider how the health of and access to health services of communities are affected by the presence of substantial numbers of uninsured residents. The institutional and economic impacts of sizable uninsured populations will be examined for particular kinds of communities (e.g., urban and rural, and with specific industrial bases).

Report 5: Economic Consequences Nationally

How much does it cost us as a nation to have roughly one out of every six or seven Americans uninsured? Who picks up the tab? Before policy makers can estimate what it may cost to change our current set of health financing arrangements, they will need a basis for comparison. In its fifth report the Committee will evaluate the costs of sustaining an uninsured population, both directly in terms of the health care provided them and indirectly in terms of their increased burden of disease and disability.

Report 6: Models and Strategies Addressing the Consequences of Uninsurance

How can communities and public and private agencies solve the problems caused by lack of coverage? In its sixth report the Committee will consider selected programs and proposals involving insurance-based strategies to expand coverage. Such strategies and models may be undertaken nationally, by states and localities, by government agencies, and by private businesses. The Committee will identify policy criteria for use in assessing the features of alternative reform strategies.

SUMMARY

Most Americans expect and receive health services when they and their families need care, but for the approximately 40 million people who have no health insurance, this is not always the reality. Health insurance is a key factor affecting whether an individual or family obtains health care. Uninsured Americans are not able to realize the benefits of American health care because they cannot obtain certain services or the services they do receive are not timely, appropriate, or well coordinated.

The most apparent deficits in care experienced by those without insurance are for chronic conditions and in preventive and screening services (Hafner-Eaton, 1993; Ayanian et al., 2000; Baker et al., 2000; Schoen and DesRoches, 2000). Far too often, key aspects of quality health care, regular care and communication with a provider to prevent and manage chronic health conditions (Institute of Medicine, 2001), are beyond the reach of uninsured persons.

As a society, we have tolerated substantial populations of uninsured persons as a residual of employment-based and public coverage since the introduction of

Medicare and Medicaid more than three and a half decades ago. Regardless of whether this result is by design or default, the consequences of our policy choices are becoming more apparent and cannot be ignored. Current public policies and insurance practices will sustain a large uninsured population under a range of projected scenarios for the national economy (Custer and Ketsche, 2000a; Fronstin, 2001). The decline in the number of uninsured people between 1997 and 1999 is not expected to continue if the economy remains slow and health care costs and insurance premiums continue to rise rapidly. By clarifying the dynamics of health insurance coverage and identifying underlying factors that contribute to unin-surance, this report and those that follow should help inform ongoing discussions about how to remedy this long-standing social problem.

NOTES

Box 1.1

This report responds to popular misperceptions about uninsured persons and populations and synthesizes recent findings regarding the dynamics of health insurance coverage and the causes of uninsurance.

- Health insurance is neither necessary nor sufficient to obtain health care, yet coverage remains one of the most important factors in obtaining access to health services. People without health insurance are much more likely than insured persons to go without needed care, including preventive services and regular care for chronic conditions, and are less likely to have a regular source of care. To the extent that these measures of access are hallmarks of quality health care, people without health insurance are at a disadvantage in obtaining high quality care.
- Americans persistently underestimate the size and diversity of the uninsured population and the potentially adverse economic and health consequences of being uninsured. During 1999, approximately 40 million people in the United States lacked health insurance coverage. Of these, almost all are under 65 years of age. More than 80 percent of uninsured children and adults under age 65 live in working families. Although working improves the chances that one and one's family will have insurance, members of families with two full-time wage earners have almost a one-in-ten chance of being uninsured.
- Most people, more than four out of five, choose to enroll in health insurance when it is offered on the job, including most lower-income workers and most young adults who work. Many of the uninsured have not been offered workplace coverage, and some who are offered a plan cannot afford the premium.
- Despite a variety of paths by which health insurance can be obtained— through employment, through individual purchase, and through public programs— a substantial proportion of the United States population continues to lack health insurance. The growth in the number of uninsured Americans has exceeded the rate of growth in the population under 65 over the past quarter century.
- Health insurance serves multiple constituencies and distinct purposes. For individuals and families, insurance is one means to promote health and plan for, if not prevent, exceptional health care costs. Providers of health care benefit from insurance as a reliable source of payment. Employers offer health benefits to attract workers and retain a satisfied and productive workforce, and communities benefit from a healthier population and stable health care institutions. The potential consequences of uninsurance vary for each of the functions of health insurance and affect different constituencies in distinct ways.
- To guide its work in future reports that will assess specific impacts, the Committee has devised a conceptual framework based on a widely used behavioral model of access to health services. This framework links the major determinants of insurance coverage with aspects of the process of obtaining health services and to potential consequences of the lack of coverage.

1

Why Health Insurance Matters

The Institute of Medicine (IOM) Committee on the Consequences of Uninsurance launches an extended examination of evidence that addresses the importance of health insurance coverage with the publication of this report. *Coverage Matters* is the first in a series of six reports that will be issued over the next two years documenting the reality and consequences of having an estimated 40 million people in the United States without health insurance coverage. These reports will examine the implications of lacking health insurance for those without it, for their families, for communities in which a substantial number of people are uninsured, and for this country as a whole.

The Committee will look at whether, where, and how the health and financial burdens of having a large uninsured population are felt, taking a broad perspective and a multidisciplinary approach to these questions. To a great extent, the costs and consequences of uninsured and unstably insured populations are hidden and difficult to measure. Financial costs incurred by those without coverage may be covered by payments for the health care of those with insurance or paid by charities and taxpayers, and the health effects may be absorbed by families in the form of diminished physical and psychological well-being, productivity, and income.

The goal of this series of studies is to refocus policy attention on a longstanding problem. Following the longest economic expansion in American history, in 1999, an estimated one out of every six Americans—32 million adults under the age of 65 and more than 10 million children—remains uninsured (Mills, 2000). A better understanding of the consequences of existing policies and health care financing arrangements should reinvigorate discussions of the issue of coverage and better equip us to design and evaluate policy initiatives and proposed reforms intended to address this problem.

The Committee's charge is to communicate to the public and policy makers analytical findings about the meaning of a large uninsured population for individuals, families, and their communities, as well as for society as a whole. Its reports should contribute to the public debate about insurance reforms and health care financing by assessing the theoretical and empirical research in health services, medicine, epidemiology, and economics that bears on the effects of lacking health insurance. It is not within the scope of this project to develop or advocate for a specific set of reforms or policies.

The goal of this first report is to provide background for the findings and conclusions that the Committee will present in subsequent reports about the consequences of uninsurance by including common definitions and an overview of the dynamics of health insurance coverage. This report addresses the extent to which Americans are without coverage, identifies social, economic, and policy factors that contribute to the existence and persistence of an uninsured population in the United States, and reports the probability for members of various population groups of being uninsured. In addition, it introduces a conceptual framework that models how health insurance affects access to health care services and, through such access, affects health and economic well-being. This framework will guide the analysis in succeeding reports in the series and will be modified to address each report's set of topics.

OBJECTIVES OF HEALTH INSURANCE COVERAGE

The first step in identifying and measuring the consequences of being without health insurance and of high uninsured rates at the community level is to recognize that the purposes and constituencies served by health insurance are multiple and distinct. These purposes include promoting health, obtaining health care for individuals and families, and protecting people financially from exceptional health care costs. Health insurance pools the risks and resources of a large group of people so that each is protected from financially disruptive medical expenses resulting from an illness, accident, or disability. In addition to serving the typical functions of risk insurance, health insurance has developed as a mechanism for financing or pre-paying a variety of health care benefits, including routine preventive services, whose use is neither rare nor unexpected. Despite the fact that a large proportion of persons with health insurance make claims against their coverage every year, health care spending, and thus health insurance payouts, remain concentrated among a relatively small number of claimants, who incur high costs for serious conditions. Ten percent of the population accounts for 70 percent of health care expenditures, a correlation that has remained constant over the past three decades (Berk and Monheit, 2001). Thus health insurance continues to serve the function of spreading risk even as it increasingly finances routine care.

From the perspective of health care providers, insurance carried by their patients helps secure a revenue stream, and communities benefit from financially viable and stable health care practitioners and institutions.

Employers offer health benefits both to attract and retain workers and to maintain a productive workforce. Government provides health insurance to populations whom the private market may not serve effectively, such as disabled and elderly persons, and populations whose access to health care is socially valued, such as children and pregnant women.

The ultimate ends of health insurance coverage for the individual and communities, including workplace communities of employees and employers, are improved health outcomes and quality of life. Attributing success in achieving these goals to health insurance alone presents a challenge because isolating the relative contribution of different determinants of individual and population health requires a complex analysis. Over the past quarter of a century, the importance of health insurance has grown, as clinical medicine has become increasingly sophisticated, technological advances have become more commonplace, and the range of therapeutic interventions (and their costs) has expanded rapidly. As a society, we invest heavily in health insurance through direct personal expenditures, forgone wages, and tax policy. Health insurance in the United States has developed as a common but not universal component of the employment contract. Employees rank health insurance first by far in importance among all the benefits offered in the workplace (Salisbury, 2001). Although there have been sizable investments of personal and public funds to provide health insurance, many people still have no coverage.

MYTHS AND REALITIES ABOUT HEALTH INSURANCE

Despite extensive reporting of survey findings and health care research results, the general public remains confused and misinformed about Americans without health insurance and the implications of lacking coverage. This section presents basic information about health insurance and who lacks it in the context of several pervasive popular myths. Without question, the complexity of American health care financing mechanisms and the wealth of sources of information add to the public's confusion and skepticism about health insurance statistics and their interpretation. This report and those that will follow aim to distill and present in readily understandable terms the extensive research that bears on questions of health insurance coverage and its importance.

Myth: **Uninsured people get health care when they really need it.** Fifty-seven percent of Americans polled in 1999 believed that those without health insurance are "able to get the care they need from doctors and hospitals" (Blendon et al., 1999, p.207). In 1993, when national attention was focused on the problems of the uninsured and on pending health care legislation, just 43 percent of those polled held this belief (Blendon et al., 1999).

Reality: **The uninsured are much more likely to forgo needed care** (Schoen and DesRoches, 2000). They also receive fewer preventive services and are less likely to have regular care for chronic conditions such as hypertension and diabetes. Chronic diseases can lead to expensive and disabling complications if they are not well managed (Lurie et al., 1984; Lurie et al., 1986; Ayanian et al., 2000). One national survey asked more than 3,400 adults about 15 highly serious or morbid conditions. Of those reporting any such symptoms (16 percent of those surveyed), and with adjustment for demographic and economic characteristics, health status, and a regular source of care,[1] an uninsured person was far less likely than someone with insurance to receive care for the reported condition (odds ratio = 0.43) (Baker et al., 2000). Additional evidence is presented later in this chapter in the discussion of insurance and access to health care.

Myth: **People without health insurance are young and healthy and choose to go without coverage.** Almost half (43 percent) of those surveyed in 2000 believed that people without health insurance are more likely to have health problems than people with insurance. About as many (47 percent) thought the likelihood of health problems is about the same for insured and uninsured people (NewsHour–Kaiser, 2000). Voters and policy makers in focus group discussions characterize those without insurance as young people who have the opportunity to be covered and feel they do not need it (Porter Novelli, 2001).

Reality: **Compared to those with at least some private coverage, the uninsured are less likely to report being in excellent or very good health** (Agency for Healthcare Research and Quality, 2001). In contrast, people reporting excellent or very good health are more likely to be insured. Among those under age 65 who are in fair or poor health, nearly one in five lacks health insurance (Rhoades and Chu, 2000). Of young adults (ages 19–34 years) in poor health, 16 percent are uninsured and 27 percent of those reporting fair health status are uninsured (Figure 1.1) (Agency for Healthcare Research and Quality, 2001).

Young adults between 19 and 34 are far more likely to lack health insurance than any other age group. This is chiefly because they are less often eligible for employment-based insurance due to the nature of their job or their short tenure in it. They are also more likely than older adults to be in excellent or very good health and consequently may forgo the cost of workplace coverage if it is offered. Turning down a workplace offer is not, however, a significant factor in explaining their lack of coverage. Younger workers accept workplace offers of coverage more often than not, and only 4 percent of all workers between 18 and 44 years of age,

---

[1]"Regular source of care" is defined as the place or provider from which one usually seeks care or advice about health care. A regular source of care may be a physician's office, a clinic, a health plan facility or a hospital emergency room or outpatient clinic. Optimally, one's regular source of care provides continuity of attention, facilitates access to appropriate services, and maintains records.

FIGURE 1.1 Probability of being uninsured for young adults, ages 19 to 34 years, by self-reported health status, 1999.
SOURCE: Center for Cost and Financing Studies, Agency for Healthcare Research and Quality, based on MEPS data.

roughly 3 million, are uninsured after turning down workplace insurance (Custer and Ketsche, 2000b). Another 11 million uninsured workers between the ages of 18 and 44 (15 percent) hold jobs that do not include an offer of coverage.

The perception that people without insurance have better-than-average health follows from confusing the relatively young age profile of the uninsured with the better health, on average, of younger persons. This obscures the link between health status and health insurance. For those without access to workplace health insurance, poor health is a potential barrier to purchasing nongroup coverage because such coverage may be highly priced, exclude preexisting conditions, or be simply unavailable. Older women (55–64 years) in the work force are especially at risk of being uninsured for this reason: 23 percent of those in good, fair, or poor health have no coverage compared to 10 percent of those in excellent or very good health (Monheit et al., 2001).

Myth: **The number of uninsured Americans is not particularly large and has not changed in recent years.** Seven out of ten respondents in a nationally representative survey thought that fewer Americans lacked health insurance than actually do (Fronstin, 1998). Roughly half (47 percent) believed that the number of people without health insurance decreased or remained constant over the latter half of the last decade (Blendon et al., 1999).

Reality: **During 1999, an estimated 42 million people in the United States lacked health insurance coverage (Mills, 2000). This number represents about 15 percent of a total population of 274 million persons. According to Census Bureau statistics, the number of Americans under** age 65 without health insurance grew from 39 million (17 percent of the population under age 65) in 1994 to 44 million (18 percent) in 1998, before falling to 42 million (17 percent) in 1999 (Fronstin, 2000d). This drop of almost 2 million in the number of people without insurance (a reduction of about 4 percent) is certainly a positive change. With a softer economy in 2000 the latest reported gains in insurance coverage may not continue (Fronstin, 2001). The decline in the number of uninsured will not continue if the economy remains slow and health care costs continue to outpace inflation. Due to the lag in measurement and reporting, however, the Census Bureau estimate of health insurance coverage for 2000 may show a further decline in the uninsured rate. This is because the data were collected for a period of strong economic performance.

Of the estimated 42 million people who were uninsured, all but about 420,000 (about 1 percent) were under 65 years of age, the age at which most Americans become eligible for Medicare;[2] 32 million were adults between ages 18 and 65, about 19 percent of all adults in this age group; and 10 million were children under 18 years of age, about 13.9 percent of all children (Mills, 2000). Throughout this report, the discussion focuses on these uninsured working-age adults and children.

These estimates of the number of persons uninsured are generated from the annual March Supplement to the Current Population Survey (CPS), conducted by the Census Bureau. Unless otherwise noted, national estimates of people without health insurance and proportions of the population with different kinds of coverage are based on the CPS, the most widely used source of estimates of insurance coverage and uninsurance rates. Seven different governmentally and privately sponsored surveys can, however, be used to make nationally representative estimates of the number of people without health insurance. These surveys and the estimates they yield are described briefly in Table B.1 in Appendix B. These surveys differ in size and sampling methods, the questions that are asked about insurance coverage, and the time period over which insurance coverage or uninsurance is measured (Lewis et al., 1998, Fronstin, 2000a). Each survey produces a different estimate of the number of Americans without insurance. The estimates range from 32 million (e.g., Medical Expenditure Panel Survey, 1996, uninsured throughout the year) to 42 million (CPS, 1999, uninsured throughout the year).[3]

The CPS has been criticized for producing estimates of persons uninsured

---

[2]Medicare, the federal insurance program for the elderly, disabled, and those with end-stage renal disease, provides almost universal coverage for hospital care for those over age 65. A small fraction of the elderly do not qualify for the program because they do not have sufficient Social Security work credits. The clergy and other religious workers comprise the largest single category of people without ties to Social Security and Medicare.

[3]In 1996, the CPS estimate of the number of nonelderly persons uninsured was 41 million (Fronstin, 2000a).

throughout the year that are too high and probably reflect periods without insurance of less than a full year as well as underreporting of Medicaid coverage (Swartz, 1986; Lewis et al., 1998; Fronstin, 2000a). The Census Bureau has recently revised its survey questionnaire to include an additional question verifying that the respondent means to report lack of coverage over the entire previous year (see Appendix B for further explanation). Still, the CPS is especially useful because it produces annual estimates relatively quickly, reporting the previous year's insurance coverage estimates each September, and because it is the basis for a consistent set of estimates for more than 20 years, allowing for analysis of trends in coverage over time. For these reasons, as well as the extensive use of the CPS in other studies of insurance coverage that are presented in this report, we rely on CPS estimates, with limitations noted. The Committee finds the variation among estimates of the number of persons uninsured produced by the different surveys less critical to its analysis than the order of magnitude of the range of estimates that these surveys yield.

The estimate of the number of uninsured people expands when a population's insurance status is tracked for several years. Over a three-year period beginning early in 1993, 72 million people, 29 percent of the U.S. population, were without coverage for at least one month. Within a single year (1994), 53 million people experienced at least a month without coverage (Bennefield, 1998a).

Myth: **Most people who lack health insurance are in nonworking families.** An April 2000 national telephone survey by the NewsHour with Jim Lehrer–Kaiser Family Foundation found that 57 percent of the adults polled believed that most people without health insurance were unemployed or from families with unemployed adults (News Hour–Kaiser, 2000). Other surveys report comparable findings (Blendon et al., 1999; Wirthlin Worldwide, 2001).

Reality: **More than 80 percent of uninsured children and adults under the age of 65 live in working families.** Six out of every ten uninsured adults are themselves employed. Although working does improve the likelihood that one and one's family members will have insurance, it is not a guarantee. Even members of families with two full-time wage earners have almost a one-in-ten chance of being uninsured (9.1 percent uninsured rate) (Hoffman and Pohl, 2000). See Chapter 3, especially Figures 3.1 and 3.2, for further details.

Myth: **New immigrants account for a substantial proportion of people without health insurance.** One analysis has attributed a significant portion of the recent growth in the size of the U.S. uninsured population to immigrants who arrived in the country between 1994 and 1998 (Camarota and Edwards, 2000).

Reality: **Recent immigrants (those who came to the United States within the past four years) do have a high rate of being uninsured (46 percent), but they and their children account for just 6 percent of those without insurance nationally** (Holahan et al., 2001). In fact, there has been a net decrease in the number of recently arrived immigrants since 1994 (Holahan et al., 2001). Overall, noncitizens account for fewer than one in five uninsured persons (Mills, 2000).

Myths and Policy Making

Popular confusion about the facts of health insurance coverage and its importance can hamper effective policy making, as can policy makers' uncertainty about the interpretation of coverage trends and consequences. This report and those that will follow aim to provide reliable information, useful to both the public and policy leaders—legislators, employers, program managers—as they meet the ongoing challenges of financing health care.

THE COMMITTEE'S ANALYTIC STRATEGY

Measuring Impacts of Coverage

Health insurance coverage is a key element in most models that depict access to health care. The relationship between health insurance and access to care is well established, as documented later in this chapter. Although the relationship between health insurance and health outcomes is neither direct nor simple, an extensive clinical and health services research literature links health insurance coverage to improved access to care, better quality, and improved personal and population health status. The Committee's conceptual framework for considering the extent and nature of these and additional effects of health insurance builds selectively upon the most widely used behavioral model of access to health services (Andersen, 1995; Andersen and Davidson 2001). The framework focuses primarily on the economic, financial, and coverage-related factors that facilitate the use of health care services. The Committee uses the framework in this introductory report to conceptualize various effects of health insurance and to provide an overview of the subsequent analyses in future reports (see Figure ES.2 and Appendix A for a further description of this model).

The Committee will use this conceptual model to identify, organize, and assess the evidence regarding important consequences of uninsurance, each of which will be the subject of a future report: individual health outcomes, family well-being, community impacts, and economic costs for society as a whole. Figure 1.2 depicts the relationship among the topics of the Committee's reports in terms of a series of overlapping circles. For example, the second report, on personal health outcomes for uninsured adults, is represented by the innermost circle of the figure, while the third report, on family well-being, encompasses the subjects of the second report but emphasizes a different unit of analysis, namely, the family. The sixth report in the series will present information about strategies and initiatives undertaken locally, statewide, or nationally to address the lack of insurance and its adverse impacts. Each of these planned reports is described briefly in Chapter 4.

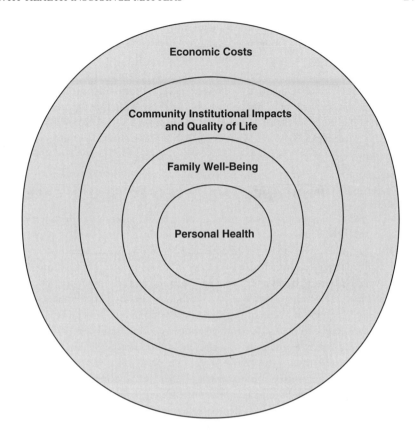

FIGURE 1.2 Levels of analysis for examining the effects of uninsurance.

Scope of This Report

This discussion of health insurance coverage focuses primarily on the U.S. population under age 65 because virtually all Americans 65 and older have Medicare or other public coverage. Furthermore, it focuses specifically on those without any health insurance for any length of time. While the effects of lacking health insurance on access to care and thus potentially on health may not be apparent for those who are uninsured only briefly, even short periods without insurance entail a measure of financial risk to self and family of incurring high expenses for health care.

The Committee does not attempt to address the condition of "underinsurance." By the "underinsured" is meant individuals or families whose health insurance policy or benefits plan offers less than adequate coverage. Most people would consider themselves underinsured if their health plan required extensive out-of-pocket payments in the form of deductibles, coinsurance or copayments, or maximum benefit limits. Many policies also exclude specific services such as mental health treatment, long-term care, or prescription drugs. The problems faced by the *under*insured are in some respects similar to those faced by the *un*insured, although they are generally less severe. *Un*insurance and *under*insurance, however, involve distinctly different policy issues, and the strategies for addressing them may differ. Throughout this study and the five reports to follow, the main focus is on persons with *no* health insurance and thus *no* assistance in paying for health care beyond what is available through charity and safety net institutions.

INSURANCE AND ACCESS TO HEALTH CARE

For individuals and families, health insurance both enhances access to health services and offers financial protection against high expenses that are relatively unlikely to be incurred as well as those that are more modest but are still not affordable to some. Health insurance is a powerful factor affecting receipt of care because both patients and physicians respond to the out-of-pocket price of services. Health insurance, however, is neither necessary nor sufficient to gain access to medical services. Nonetheless, the independent and direct effect of health insurance coverage on access to health services is well established. This section documents that research literature and presents the Committee's findings regarding access to care.

Subsequent Committee reports will build on this finding and evaluate evidence for the further relationship between insurance coverage and health outcomes. Appendix A describes and depicts schematically the Committee's conceptual model of this complex relationship, which is affected by a variety of personal, economic, and social factors and health care processes that are in turn subject to many influences.

Health Insurance Facilitates Access to Care

Many people who lack health insurance will forgo the care they need until their condition becomes intolerable. Others will obtain the health care they need even without health insurance, by paying for it out of pocket or seeking it from providers who offer care free or at highly subsidized rates. For still others, health insurance alone does not ensure receipt of care because of other nonfinancial barriers, such as a lack of health care providers in their community, limited access to transportation, illiteracy, or linguistic and cultural differences. Nonetheless, health insurance remains a key factor in assuring access to health care.

Formal research about uninsured populations in the United States dates to the late 1920s and early 1930s when the Committee on the Cost of Medical Care produced a series of reports about financing physician office visits and hospitalizations. This issue became salient as the numbers of medically indigent climbed during the Great Depression. With the rise of commercial insurers and the decline of community rating offered by Blue Cross–Blue Shield and other nonprofit insurers in the 1950s, new studies of individual and family health expenditures were co-sponsored by the University of Chicago and the Health Information Foundation. These studies became the factual basis for legislation that was enacted as the Medicare and Medicaid amendments to the Social Security Act in 1965.

Since the enactment of Medicare and Medicaid, health services research on uninsured populations has been sponsored federally and privately, at increasing levels of support over time and using new survey tools and data sets (Somers and Somers, 1961; Numbers, 1979; Starr, 1982; Andersen and Anderson, 1999). The Census Bureau started collecting detailed information about health insurance in the latter half of the 1970s and the National Center for Health Services Research, a predecessor to AHRQ, conducted the National Medical Care Expenditure Survey (NMCES) in 1977, followed by the National Medical Expenditure Survey (NMES) in 1987 and AHRQ's Medical Expenditure Panel Survey (MEPS), launched and conducted annually since 1996. A summary of the major surveys collecting health insurance and utilization information is presented in Appendix B.

Population-based surveys have been used to examine access to health services by measuring components of primary care, such as number of physician visits and immunization rates, sites of care (e.g., physician office, hospital outpatient department, clinic), barriers to care (e.g., inability to pay), and unmet health needs (e.g., health status, inability to obtain care when needed) (Andersen and Aday, 1978; Aday et al., 1984; Lurie et al., 1984; Monheit et al., 1985; Lurie et al., 1986; Hafner-Eaton, 1993; Newacheck et al., 1993; Himmelstein and Woolhandler, 1995; Sox et al., 1998; Hsia et al., 2000; Kasper et al., 2000). The likelihood of having any physician visit within a year, the number of visits annually, and having a regular source of care are well established measures of access. Empirical studies consistently support the link between access to care and improved health outcomes (Bindman et al., 1995; Starfield, 1995).

Having a regular source of care can be considered a *predictor* of access, rather than a direct measure of it, when health outcomes are themselves used as access indicators. This extension of the notion of access measurement was made by the IOM Committee on Monitoring Access to Personal Health Care Services (Millman, 1993, p.33):

> "[T]he committee defined access as follows: the timely use of personal health services to achieve the best possible health outcomes. Importantly, this definition relies on both the use of health services and health outcomes to provide yardsticks for judging whether access has been achieved."

Thus, in *Access to Health Care in America*, the earlier IOM committee incorporated health outcomes into the definition of access. In this first report of the Committee on the Consequences of Uninsurance, consideration of the relationship between health insurance and access is limited to well established findings regarding *process* measures of access. The next report, which will examine health outcomes for the uninsured, will evaluate clinical and epidemiological research evidence in terms of the more demanding concept of *realized* access to health care.

The likelihood that those without health insurance lack a regular source of care has increased substantially since 1977. In 1996, people without insurance were 2.5 times more likely to lack a regular source of care than were the insured (Zuvekas and Weinick, 1999; Weinick et al., 2000). Children without insurance were three times as likely as children with Medicaid coverage to have no regular source of care (15 percent versus 5 percent), and uninsured adults were more than three times as likely as either privately or publicly insured adults to lack a regular source of care (35 percent versus 11 percent) (Haley and Zuckerman, 2000).

The benefits for children of having health insurance and a regular source of care, in terms of routine physician visits and appropriate preventive care, are well documented (Lave et al., 1998; Newacheck et al., 1998; Haley and Zuckerman, 2000). However, the impact of parents' health and health insurance on the well-being of their children has received attention only recently. Whether or not parents are insured appears to affect whether or not their children receive care—as well as how much care—even if the children themselves have coverage (Hanson, 1998). The health of parents can affect their ability to care for their children and the level of family stress. Worrying about their children's access to care is itself a source of stress for parents.

Uninsured adults are less likely to receive health services, even for certain serious conditions. In a study described earlier (Baker et al., 2000), even after adjusting for differences in age, sex, income, and health status, uninsured people were less than half as likely as insured persons to receive care for a condition that physicians deemed highly serious and requiring medical attention. People without insurance are also less likely than people with insurance to receive preventive services and appropriate routine care for chronic conditions, even as the importance of preventive care and the prevalence of chronic disease become more prominent elements within health care (Hafner-Eaton, 1993; Ayanian et al., 2000; Institute of Medicine, 2001). Finally, those who lack health insurance are more likely to be hospitalized for conditions that might have been avoided with timely ambulatory care (Weissman et al., 1992; Kozak et al., 2001).

The level of out-of-pocket costs for care has been demonstrated in randomized trials, natural experiments, and observational studies to have substantial effects on the use of health care services (Newhouse et al., 1993; Zweifel and Manning, 2000). Table 1.1 gives a sense of the magnitude of these costs. Uninsured patients may be charged more than patients with coverage, who benefit from discounts negotiated by their insurer, which amplifies the financial impact of lacking coverage (Wielawski, 2000; Kolata, 2001).

Differential Access to Care for the Uninsured

Not only do persons without insurance receive less care, but the providers who serve them differ systematically from those who treat insured patients. Public hospitals, health departments, and health clinics (e.g., community, migrant, or rural health centers) are more likely than other providers to serve uninsured

TABLE 1.1 Illustrative Charges to Patients, Insured and Uninsured, 1999[a] (in dollars)

	Physician Office Visit	Normal Hospital Delivery (Childbirth)	Hospital, Simple Pneumonia (Adult)
Fee for service[b]		100–1,590	100–3,434
Before deductible is met	62		
After deductible is met	6		
Managed care plan	10	0	0
No insurance	62	4,543	9,812

[a]These illustrative charges are based on policies offered under the Federal Employees Health Benefits Program plans in 2001 and on national average actual charges to Mutual of Omaha health insurance policy holders for 1999 (Office of Personnel Management, *http://www.opm.gov;* Mutual of Omaha, *http://www.mutualofomaha.com/acrodocs/group/mug6440.pdf*).

[b]Annual deductibles range from $100-$500 per person; coinsurance rates for outpatient services are 10% if preferred providers are used, 20–35% for other providers.

persons, two-thirds of whom are members of lower-income families (annual income below 200 percent of the federal poverty level [FPL]: $33,400 for a family of four in 1999). These institutions generally receive public funding to support the provision of free or reduced fee care to those who cannot afford to pay private fees. They serve as "core safety-net providers," with two distinguishing characteristics:

"(1) either by legal mandate or explicitly adopted mission they maintain an "open door," offering access to services for patients regardless of their ability to pay; and (2) a substantial share of their patient mix is uninsured, Medicaid, and other vulnerable patients" (Institute of Medicine, 2000).

The IOM report on the safety net also stressed the diversity of local safety-net providers and services across states, communities, and geographic regions. In rural areas, for instance, the mix of safety-net providers tends to feature private physicians and health centers or clinics, whereas urban areas are more likely to be served by teaching hospitals (Schur and Franco, 1999).

In addition to those providers whose patient populations include substantial proportions of uninsured persons, in the aggregate, private physicians, community hospitals, and teaching hospitals affiliated with academic health centers provide significant amounts of care to uninsured patients (Cunningham and Tu, 1997; Mann et al., 1997; Institute of Medicine, 2000). Nationally representative surveys show that between two-thirds and three-quarters of physicians report providing some charity care, accounting for about 5 percent of their case load on average (Foreman, 1992; Cunningham, 1999b).

The wide geographic variation in the organization, financing, and delivery of health services contributes to the scarcity of quantitative information about services for uninsured people. Compared with insured persons, greater numbers of uninsured persons obtain care from hospitals and clinics or health centers than from office-based physicians, and are less likely to identify a person, rather than a facility, as their usual source of care (Shi, 2000a). Uninsured patients are less than half as likely as insured patients to report that a physician's office is their usual source of care (about one-third of all uninsured patients compared with about two-thirds of the general population) (Cunningham and Whitmore, 1998).

Hospital emergency departments or outpatient departments serve as the regular source of care for one out of every six uninsured patients that report having a regular source of care (Weinick et al., 1997). A substantial proportion of emergency department visits is for nonurgent conditions (Pane et al., 1991; Grumbach et al., 1993; Baker et al., 1994; Zimmerman et al., 1996). Because hospital emergency departments are legally required to assess and stabilize all patients with any medical condition without regard for ability to pay, they are the only providers who cannot turn uninsured patients away for lack of a source of payment.[4] Although emergency departments are portrayed as a costly and inappropriate site of primary care services, many uninsured patients seek care in emergency departments because they are sent there by other health care providers or have nowhere else to go. Emergency care specialists argue that the nation's emergency departments not only serve as providers of last resort but are a critical entry point into the health care system (O'Brien et al., 1999).

WHAT FOLLOWS

Three chapters follow in this report. Chapter 2 provides an overview of how employment-based health insurance, public programs and individual insurance policies operate and interact to provide extensive but incomplete coverage of the U.S. population. This includes a review of historical trends and public policies affecting both public and private insurance, a discussion of the interactions among the different types of insurance, and an examination of why people move from one program to another or end up with no coverage.

Chapter 3 synthesizes existing information to arrive at a composite description of the uninsured: What characteristics do people without coverage often share? Where do the uninsured live? The chapter also presents information about the risk of being or becoming uninsured: How does the chance of being uninsured change depending on selected characteristics, such as racial and ethnic identity, rural or urban residency, and age? What are the probabilities for specific popula-

---

[4]The federal Emergency Medical Treatment and Active Labor Act, part of the Consolidated Omnibus Budget Reconciliation Act of 1985, requires hospital emergency rooms to assess and stabilize all patients with a life- or limb-threatening or emergency medical condition or those who are about to give birth. Hospitals are not required to provide continuing care after the patient has been stabilized and transferred or released. No federal funds directly support this mandate.

tions, such as racial and ethnic minorities, rural residents, and older working-age persons, of being uninsured? How does the chance of being uninsured change over a lifetime?

In addition to characterizing the likelihood of being uninsured in terms of a single dimension, such as gender, age, race, work status, or geographic region, Chapter 3 also presents the results of multivariate analyses that offer a more informative depiction of the factors that contribute to the chances of being uninsured.

Finally, in Chapter 4 the Committee presents the research agenda for its overall project and previews the five future reports.

Box 2.1

In the United States, health insurance is a voluntary matter, yet many people are involuntarily without coverage. There is no guarantee for most people under the age of 65 that they will be eligible for or able to afford to purchase or retain health insurance.

• Almost seven out of every ten Americans* under age 65 years are covered by employment-based health insurance, either from their job or through a parent or spouse. Three quarters of workers are offered health insurance by their employers, and most decide to purchase or take up the offer of coverage. Of the 17 percent of workers who decline an employer's offer, about a quarter, or 4 percent of workers overall, remain uninsured.

• Individually purchased policies and public insurance (primarily Medicaid) together cover one out of five persons under age 65.* Both have limitations. Poor health status or low income may preclude the purchase of an affordable individual policy. The combination of strict eligibility requirements and complex enrollment procedures makes public coverage often difficult to obtain and even more difficult to maintain over time.

• A change in insurance premium or terms, as well as changes in income, health, marital status, terms of employment, or public policies, can trigger a loss or gain of health insurance coverage. For about one-third of the uninsured population, being without coverage is a temporary or one-time interruption of coverage, and the median duration of a period without insurance is between 5 and 6 months. Uninsured persons in low-income families and those with less education experience longer periods without coverage, on average, than their higher income and more educated counterparts.

• Insurance industry underwriting practices, the costs of health services, and the patchwork of public policies regarding insurance coverage all contribute to the economic pressures on employers, insurers, and government programs offering health insurance. Small firms are especially likely to face high costs. Workers who take up an employer's offer of a subsidized health benefit typically pay directly between one-quarter and one-third of the total cost of their insurance premium, in addition to paying deductibles, copayments, and the costs of health services that are not covered or are covered only in part by their health plan. For families earning less than 200 percent of the federal poverty level, these expenses can exceed 10 percent of their annual income.

• Since the mid-1970s, growth in the cost of health insurance has outpaced the rise in real income, creating a gap in purchasing ability that has added roughly one million persons to the ranks of the uninsured each year. Despite the economic prosperity of recent years, between 1998 and 1999 there was only a slight drop in the numbers and proportion of uninsured Americans. Through the early 1990s, the rising uninsured rate reflected a decline in employment-based coverage. Since the mid-1990s, increases in employment-based coverage have been offset by steady or declining rates of public and individually purchased coverage.

---

* Altogether, about 83 percent of the nonelderly population is covered by employment-based, individual and public plans. Some people report more than one source of coverage over the course of a year.

2

The Dynamics of Health
Insurance Coverage

This chapter provides an overview of the conditions under which people acquire, maintain, and lose health insurance coverage in the United States. Understanding that health insurance status can change over time and that the risk of being uninsured changes over the course of a lifetime is critical for identifying and evaluating the consequences of uninsurance.

In this chapter, the Committee considers the dynamic and unstable nature of health insurance coverage, which results in large numbers of uninsured Americans. It opens with a brief discussion of the sources of health insurance coverage and the role of health benefits as part of an employee's compensation package. Federal and state policies create the economic and political environments within which opportunities for coverage are created and accepted or declined. Next the Committee lays out the mechanisms through which people gain and lose coverage, with attention to the considerations that frame decision making about offering and taking up an offer of private or public coverage. Lastly, the chapter considers the coverage trends over time for both private and public insurance.

NO GUARANTEE OF COVERAGE

In the United States, there is no guarantee for most people under the age of 65 that they will be eligible for, able to afford the purchase of, or able to stay enrolled in a health insurance plan.[1] American social values contain a

---

[1]The Committee distinguishes health insurance from programs and institutions whose missions include providing health services directly to those who lack other sources of financial coverage for this

deeply rooted tension with respect to health care. In one respect, health care is viewed as a market commodity, whose efficiency of production and consumption depends on the discipline of market forces. Alternatively, health care is understood to be a social good, something that all members of our society should be able to obtain when they need it. This tension has contributed to the varied and complex set of arrangements to finance the delivery of health services that has developed incrementally in response to specific populations and problems with access to health care (Stevens, 1989; Stone, 1993). As a result of this piecemeal approach, about 40 million Americans find themselves without insurance coverage each year, and millions more are uninsured at some point when measured over longer periods of time (Bennefield, 1998a; Mills, 2000).

Health insurance in the United States is a voluntary matter, yet many people are involuntarily without coverage. The cost of coverage limits feasible options for most individuals and families. Employers and government agencies also must make strategic choices about whether and how much coverage to offer. In addition, the underwriting and marketing practices of the insurance industry further limit—and at times eliminate—options.

Within the private sector, coverage depends on an employer's decision to offer a health benefit plan and an employee's decision to enroll or take up this offer. Employers (and unions) decide whether to sponsor health benefits for some or all of their work force (on the basis of work status or occupation), how much to subsidize each worker's insurance premium (if at all), and whether to self-insure or purchase coverage from a third party. Federal tax policy provides incentives but no mandate for employers to offer insurance coverage and for employees to purchase coverage through an employment-based plan. Eighty-four percent of all employers offered a health insurance plan to at least some of their employees, and 76 percent of all workers (excluding dependents) were offered the option to participate in an employment-based plan (Fronstin, 2001). Most employees offered coverage choose to accept (83 percent) and to pay their portion of the insurance premium, resulting in an overall rate of 63 percent of all workers insured through their employment-based plan (Fronstin, 2001).

When workers are not offered the option to purchase employment-based insurance for themselves and their dependent family members (spouses and minor children), or if they decline to enroll, they may have no other alternatives for coverage. Insurance companies may refuse to sell a policy to someone in poor health, or the premiums may be unaffordable. Thirty-two percent of all members

---

care, such as public clinics and hospitals, community health centers, and emergency departments. Similarly, it does not consider the facilities and services of the Indian Health Service, which provide care to entitled American Indians (members of federally recognized tribes), or those of the Department of Veterans Affairs, which serve veterans entitled to care because of military service and disability, to constitute health insurance. Access or entitlement to care that is not portable, even in the case of urgent or emergency care, is not considered "health insurance" as the term is used in this report.

of working families (roughly 40 million people) are not offered health insurance by the employer of the family's primary wage earner (Custer and Ketsche, 2000b, using 1996 data from the Medical Expenditure Panel Survey). Among those who decline a workplace offer of insurance (17 percent), only about a quarter remain uninsured because most obtain coverage through a spouse's policy. For members of families who are not offered workplace coverage, the residual uninsured rate is much higher, at 45 percent (Custer and Ketsche, 2000b).

Public insurance programs fill some but not all of the coverage gaps created by the employment-based approach to health insurance coverage. Participation in public insurance such as Medicaid and the State Children's Health Insurance Program (SCHIP) hinges on eligibility, which is means-tested and limited to specific categories of people—for example, children and pregnant women, and people certified as having a permanent disabling condition. Except for Part A of the federal Medicare program (hospital insurance), which ensures coverage of almost all persons 65 years and older, an individual's participation in publicly sponsored health insurance is optional.

The federally sponsored Medicaid program and SCHIP are structured as options for states and eligible individuals. States may receive federal matching funds by establishing a program that fulfills certain national eligibility, benefit, and reimbursement standards, or they may forgo federal dollars if they choose not to administer programs that meet these federal standards. All of the states have chosen to operate both types of programs, and each state determines its own income and other eligibility criteria within federal statutory limits. One result of the historical connection between Medicaid and income support programs for low income families with children has been that coverage rates for childless low income adults have lagged behind those for children. The enrollment of eligible children in Medicaid and SCHIP has been hindered by administrative complexities and a lack of effective communication with parents about their children's potential eligibility (Perry et al., 2000; Kronebusch, 2001).

OPPORTUNITIES FOR OBTAINING COVERAGE

Almost seven out of ten Americans under age 65 years (66 percent) are covered by employment-based health insurance, either from their job or from that of their parent or spouse (Fronstin, 2000d). Individually purchased policies and public insurance together account for another 21 percent of coverage, and 17 percent of the general population remains without any coverage throughout the year (Figure 2.1).[2]

Obtaining coverage and staying insured can be a challenging proposition for

---

[2]These fractions add to more than 100 percent because some people have coverage from more than one source during the course of a year, for example, Medicaid for some months and a workplace policy at another time.

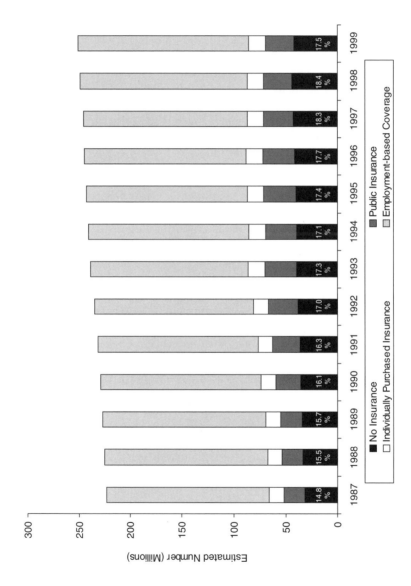

FIGURE 2.1 Sources of health insurance coverage for persons under age 65 years, 1987–1999.
SOURCE: Fronstin, 2000d.

individuals and families. Eligibility, enrollment, and maintenance of enrollment depend on complex and interdependent considerations related to the labor market, the health services market, and population demographic (Figure 2.2). Especially for those who do not obtain employment-based coverage, the paths that lead to enrolling and staying enrolled in a health plan include potential barriers to coverage.

Employment-Based Insurance Covers Two-Thirds of the Population Under Age 65

Most Americans under age 65 obtain health insurance through their employers or as the dependent spouse or child of a wage earner with employment-based coverage. Employment-based health benefits plans became more common in the 1940s and until the mid-1970s the proportion of the population covered by health insurance rose, at times dramatically (Starr, 1982; Numbers, 1985). Since the mid-1970s, however, the growth of per capita health services spending has outstripped growth in personal income (real wages) and revealed the limits of employment-based coverage.

The rising cost of health insurance policies has become prohibitive for some employers and workers, particularly those in small firms, and for employees at lower wage levels (Kronick and Gilmer, 1999). In the midst of the recent economic boom and low unemployment, the proportion of small- to medium-sized firms (3–199 employees) offering health insurance actually rose, from 54 to 67 percent (Fronstin, 2001). These gains, however, are vulnerable not only to the general state of the economy but also to continued increases in premiums (Fronstin, 2001).

Virtually all large employers offer health benefits to at least some of their workforce. Health insurance gives them a way to offer a tax-subsidized benefit that employees value enough to forgo a higher salary or income. Further, employers can take advantage of economies of scale and risk pooling to provide this group health benefit, which employees cannot match on their own. Employers respond to a variety of considerations when deciding whether to offer health benefits to their workers and under what terms the offer will be made. The price of coverage is critical to the employer's decision. The annual total cost for an average health policy at work is $2,426 for individual and $6,351 for family coverage in 2000. This represents a cost of doing business that is influenced by federal tax policies, regional health services markets, and the underwriting practices and vitality of regional and local insurance markets.

When a firm provides a health insurance benefit, it may choose to withhold it from some of its employees. Some firms offer the benefit only to employees who work full-time or have been with the firm for a minimum period. Workers who are not offered health insurance in the workplace tend to have lower educational attainment (high-school diploma or less), to hold a low-wage or nonunion job,

40

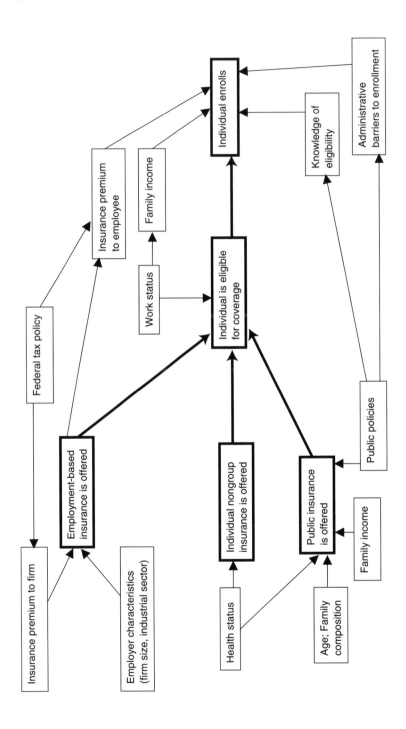

FIGURE 2.2 Factors affecting eligibility and enrollment.
NOTE: Bold lines indicate major pathways and decision points.

and to be employed in a temporary, part-time, or contract position (Custer and Ketsche 2000b; Farber and Levy, 2000, Gabel, 1999).

The employee's share of the insurance premium does not represent the full cost to the worker of health insurance. According to the economic theory of compensating differentials, the wage level required to attract workers will be lower when employers provide subsidized health insurance than it would be if employers did not offer a subsidy. As a result, economists expect that workers implicitly "pay" for at least part of their health insurance subsidy by receiving lower wages than they would otherwise receive (Currie and Madrian, 1999).

Individual Policies Fill Part of the Coverage Gap

Health insurance purchased by individuals outside the employment-based group context is, on average, more expensive to obtain, less consistent a product due to a varied mix of offerings, and unavailable to many people who are, as one recent study concluded, in "less-than-perfect health" (Pollitz et al., 2001). About 16 million children and working-age adults were covered by individually issued, nongroup policies in 1999, or almost 7 percent of the population under age 65 (Fronstin, 2000d). Substantial numbers of enrollees are drawn from the self-employed and agricultural workers, persons who retire before becoming eligible for Medicare, part-time and contingent workers, those who lose coverage through a spouse, and young adults who grow too old to be covered under a parent's health coverage (Pollitz et al., 2001; GAO, 1996). While 30 to 40 percent of these enrollees participate for less than a year, to fill coverage gaps created by a change in economic or other life circumstances, over half of those who purchase individual policies do so as a more permanent source of coverage (Chollet and Kirk, 1998).

Premiums for insurance purchased through a small group or the individual market are more expensive, on average, than employment-based coverage.[3] A combination of adverse selection (the greater-than-average likelihood that individuals and families with health problems will purchase coverage rather than be uninsured), lesser precision in predicting expenditures due to the small size of the risk pool, and higher administrative costs make the "loading factor" (premiums

---

[3]One study, for example, assumes that the premium cost for individually purchased coverage is 20 percent greater than the employee's cost for employment-based coverage (Gabel et al., 1998). The authors estimate that single coverage purchased on the individual market would cost 32 percent of the pre-tax annual income of someone whose earnings were less than 100 percent of FPL and family coverage would cost 41 percent. For persons earning 200 percent of FPL, individually purchased coverage would cost 16 percent of pre-tax income for single coverage and 20 percent for a family of four. A more recent study of the individual market found a national average premium for single coverage to be $333 per month, or about $4,000 annually (Pollitz et al., 2001).

charged minus benefits paid out, divided by premiums) higher for individual policies than for group insurance (Gabel et al., 1998; Pauly and Percy, 2000). Reflecting the relatively high premiums for this source of coverage, more than half of the population covered under individually purchased insurance live in families with incomes higher than 300 percent of the federal poverty level (FPL), or $50,100 for a family of four in 1999 (Chollet and Kirk, 1998).

Some applicants are priced out of the market for individual coverage. Medical underwriting practices applied to individual applicants for nongroup coverage mean that, compared with employment-based coverage, eligibility is more sensitive to an applicant's health status, age, family income, and geographic area of residence (Chollet and Kirk, 1998). For example, one recent study of eight nongroup insurance markets found that the premium price for individual policies was increased by 38 percent for persons with health problems, compared with a price quote for a person without health problems (Pollitz et al., 2001). In addition, most states allow risk rating for age, which means that individual policies tend to be steeply price adjusted by age, making individual policies relatively expensive for older people (Chollet and Kirk, 1998; Blue Cross Blue Shield, 2000).

Federal and state reforms of the small group and individual markets have restricted the use of medical underwriting to exclude applicants from eligibility, although these reforms usually do not restrict the premium prices that may be charged for such coverage and in some cases have resulted in increased premium prices (Pollitz et al., 2001). The Health Insurance Portability and Accountability Act of 1996 (HIPAA) establishes certain rights to individually purchased coverage for a limited group of eligible persons who formerly were covered by employment-based plans (Nichols and Blumberg, 1998). However, there is no regulation of the premiums that insurers may charge HIPAA-eligible individuals.

Another HIPAA requirement, that an insurance product be guaranteed to be available to all, regardless of health status (so-called guaranteed issue), has been accompanied in some states by premium rating reforms. But even these reforms only partially address insurers' reluctance to incur adverse risk selection (Hall, 2000; Swartz, 2000). In a study of seven states where reforms to minimize the impact of health status on rates included rating bands and modified or pure community rating, insurers responded by dividing small groups into blocks of business to re-introduce medical underwriting indirectly, by means of rate adjustments allowed for distinguishing differences in benefits, age, the family size to be covered, and geographic location (Hall, 2000).

The individual market may limit benefits for or exclude persons with chronic health conditions, for example, persons who are HIV positive, have survived a bout with cancer, or who live with diabetes, heart disease, or asthma (GAO, 1996). Some 29 states operate or regulate insurance programs that maintain high risk pools to cover limited numbers of uninsured residents whose poor health status puts them at higher-than-average risk for incurring large health care costs and for whom individually purchased coverage would otherwise be inaccessible (Wolman, 1992; GAO, 1996). However, there are waiting lists or closed enrollments for many of these pools, and premiums may be as high as 150 to 200 percent of the price for individually purchased coverage. Nationally, risk pools enroll approximately 100,000 persons, about half of this number in California and Minnesota alone (Pollitz et al., 2001).

Public Insurance Fills Part of the Coverage Gap

In the 1960s, creation of the basic federal Medicare program for seniors and the shared federal and state Medicaid programs for specific categories of the poor brought health insurance coverage to many of those who had been excluded from the employment-based approach to financing health services delivery (Starr, 1982). Individuals who are at least 65 years of age and have worked for at least 10 years in Medicare-covered employment (or whose spouse has), the permanently and totally disabled, and those with end-stage renal disease are eligible for Medicare. Individual eligibility for Medicare depends on age, and for a relatively small proportion of those covered, on disability or health status. Medicare provides virtually universal coverage for hospital and outpatient medical services for those over 65.

Qualifying to participate in Medicaid or SCHIP involves fulfilling requirements related to income and assets (making these so-called means-tested programs) and being a member of a specific group that is eligible for benefits, for example, pregnant women, minor children, the elderly, and some of the permanently disabled. Those who meet economic and group criteria must also meet immigration status and residency requirements. Eligibility standards vary by state, with general oversight provided by the federal government. Medicaid covers approximately 41 million people, of whom about half are under the age of 21 and between 13 million and 14 million are parents and disabled adults under age 65 (Health Care Financing Administration, 2001, 1998 data). Thus, Medicaid covers approximately 15 percent of the population under age 65 for at least part of each year. Medicaid also provides supplemental benefits for about 5 million low-income Medicare beneficiaries.

Federal welfare reform legislation passed in 1996 severed the connection between eligibility for income benefits, such as Aid to Families with Dependent Children (AFDC) and Supplemental Security Income (SSI), and Medicaid coverage. Although this reform was not intended to reduce the number of persons enrolled in Medicaid, it has had that effect (Broaddus and Ku, 2000; Cunningham and Park, 2000; Holahan and Kim, 2000; Kronebusch, 2001). By mid-1997, almost half of women and 30 percent of children were uninsured a year or more after leaving welfare (Garrett and Holahan, 2000). SCHIP, federally authorized in 1997, with implementation beginning in some states the following year, has begun to reduce the numbers of children who are uninsured. Medicaid enrollments have also begun to increase, according to administrative data. The latest figures show an increase in the number of children and adult Medicaid enrollees under age 65 of more than 8 million persons, from 25 million in 1997 to 33 million in 1998 (HCFA, 2001).

Interaction of Private and Public Insurance

Employment-based coverage and public insurance programs are not explicitly coordinated, yet they influence one another, particularly in periods of economic change. Medicaid eligibility expansions since the late 1980s have offset some, but not all, of the decline in employment-based insurance coverage that occurred before 1994 (Holahan and Kim, 2000). Without these Medicaid expansions, it is estimated that an additional 11 million people would have been uninsured (Carrasquillo et al., 1999a).

With expansions of Medicaid eligibility and the implementation of SCHIP, a certain percentage of uninsured persons who were eligible for employment-based health insurance, and insured persons who had such coverage, may have chosen to enroll in public insurance instead. In addition, some employers may have been less likely to offer dependent coverage to their lower-waged workers, knowing that publicly subsidized insurance was available for children. The extent of this so-called "crowding out" or substitution of privately purchased coverage by public insurance has been estimated in a number of studies, none of which is fully comparable in terms of methods, data sources, or questions asked (Alteras, 2001; Cutler and Gruber, 1997; Dubay, 1999). For the Medicaid expansions, early estimates of crowd-out approaching 50 percent (Cutler and Gruber, 1996 a,b) have been challenged on methodological grounds. More recent estimates have been as low as 4 percent, with upper bounds between 17 percent and 23 percent, depending on how crowd-out is defined and measured (Alteras, 2001; Cutler and Gruber, 1997; Blumberg et al., 2000; Dubay, 1999; Thorpe and Florence, 1998; Yazici and Kaestner, 2000).

Evidence of the substitution or "crowd-out" of private insurance by public insurance has informed public policy debates about the importance of balancing potentially negative outcomes of expanded eligibility for public insurance with positive outcomes including increased enrollment in insurance, particularly for children; decreased financial pressure on lower-income family budgets; and an improved level of covered benefits for working families (Alteras, 2001; Dubay and Kenney, 2001; Lutzsky and Hill, 2001; Swartz, 1996). For example, in the case of SCHIP, there is concern not to single out for unfair treatment those families who have valued coverage highly enough to purchase coverage for their children at a high cost, by denying them entry into publicly subsidized insurance (Swartz, 1996).

Popular belief that Medicaid expansions resulted in a substantial crowding out of employment-based coverage has influenced the design and functioning of SCHIP, reflecting a tension between efforts to diminish substitution while boosting enrollment (Lutzsky and Hill, 2001). The Balanced Budget Act of 1997, which created SCHIP, and the federal regulations that guide implementation both address crowd-out directly, given the expectation of more substitution at SCHIP's higher income eligibility levels and with planned SCHIP expansions to include eligibility for parents and possible subsidy of employment-based insurance premiums. Federal regulations require state planning to minimize crowd-out and regulation of plans to subsidize employment-based insurance premiums (Lutzsky and Hill, 2001). State responses have included waiting periods (the most common, about two-thirds of all states), screening to determine whether applicants are eligible for private insurance, cost-sharing (e.g., premiums for families above 150 percent FPL) where SCHIP is not part of Medicaid, and direct regulation of insurers or employers (Lutzky and Hill, 2001). In some states, there are exceptions made for situations where employment-based insurance premiums are unaffordable or when individuals or families experience a change in insurance or economic status (Lutzsky and Hill, 2001).

Since 1997, concern about SCHIP substituting for or crowding out employment-based coverage has diminished and the limits of experience with Medicaid expansions in predicting the future of SCHIP have been acknowledged. Many public officials have concluded that crowd-out is not an issue for families earning less than 150 percent of FPL, and just 3 to 8 percent of SCHIP applicants are turned down because they were eligible for private coverage or enrolled in private coverage (Lutzsky and Hill, 2001).

Public Policies Shape the Marketplace for Health Insurance

Federal tax policy gives favorable treatment to employment-based health insurance.[4] The employer's share of the premium is excluded from the employee's taxable income. If the firm has a qualified flexible benefit plan, employees can pay their share of the premium with pre-tax dollars. Recent federal tax legislative reforms now allow self-employed people to claim a deduction for a share of their health insurance premiums, and full deductibility of the premiums of self-employed workers is being phased in. For the year 2000, the exclusion of employer contributions from both federal income and Social Security taxes, together with smaller exemptions and deductions for health care spending from personal income taxes, resulted in a federal subsidy estimated at $125.6 billion (Sheils et al., 1999). This represents a sizable federal expenditure for the support of employment-based health insurance. Since most state income taxes are based on the federal income tax structure, state taxes also subsidize employment-based health benefits.

To the extent that employers pay premiums for their employees' health benefits instead of cash wages, this business expense to the employer is a form of

---

[4]Workplace health benefits and the subsidies paid by employers for premium costs were a response to wage and price controls imposed on industry during World War II, when health benefits were provided in lieu of wage increases. In 1954, the Internal Revenue Services codified the exemption of employer-paid health benefits from employee taxable income (Starr, 1982).

tax-free income to the employee. This tax subsidy benefits families with high incomes more than those with low incomes because the amount of the subsidy is related directly to an individual's tax rate and those with higher incomes face higher marginal tax rates. In 2000, families with annual incomes greater than $100,000 had an average federal tax subsidy resulting from the employer's payment of the insurance premium of $2,638, while the average subsidy for families with incomes of less than $15,000 was $79 (Figure 2.3) (Sheils et al., 1999).

At the state level, most insurance regulation concerns the individually purchased and small-group health insurance market rather than policies offered by large private-sector employers. The Employee Retirement Income Security Act of 1974 (ERISA) mandates that certain group health benefits offered through the workplace be considered under federal pension law rather than state insurance regulations (EBRI, 2000). One recent change in this pattern of jurisdiction lies in the federal Health Insurance Portability and Accountability Act of 1996 (HIPAA), which has resulted in most states providing guaranteed issue of at least one health insurance plan, guaranteeing renewal for certain policy holders in all states, and restricting preexisting condition exclusions by statute for individuals who are leaving employment-based plans (HIPAA-eligible persons) (Chollet and Kirk, 1998). Fourteen states require that insurers guarantee the issue of at least one product to all applicants, although some of these states impose restrictions on qualified applicants. Eighteen states have imposed some kind of limitations on variations in premiums or prohibited the use of certain rating factors such as age, gender, claims experience, or health status (Pauly and Percy, 2000).

HOW PEOPLE GAIN AND LOSE COVERAGE

Many conventional and economic transitions over the course of a lifetime can result in a loss of health insurance coverage for a person or family because income, health status, marital status, and terms of employment can influence eligibility for and participation in health insurance. An illness or accident serious enough to interrupt work and income, the loss of one's job, divorce from or death of a spouse whose employment provided family health benefits, or retirement from work before age 65 (when Medicare eligibility begins) can result in the loss of insurance. When children reach age 18 or leave college, they usually lose public benefits or coverage under their parent's health insurance plan. Increasing one's income, even if barely above the eligibility limit, may result in a total loss of Medicaid coverage, even if workplace health benefits are not available or affordable. Some people, after a gap in coverage, cannot purchase individual insurance at any price because of preexisting health conditions. Conversely, many of these same transitional events are accompanied by increased opportunities for insurance coverage. For example, marriage can make dependents eligible for an employment-based plan, death of a father or divorce might make the widow and children eligible for Medicaid, and a major disabling accident could lead to eligibility for Medicare's program for the disabled (Figure 2.4).

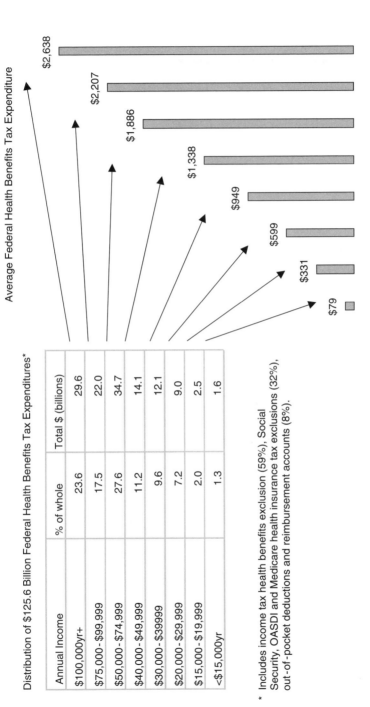

Average Federal Health Benefits Tax Expenditure

Distribution of $125.6 Billion Federal Health Benefits Tax Expenditures*

Annual Income	% of whole	Total $ (billions)
$100,000yr+	23.6	29.6
$75,000 - $99,999	17.5	22.0
$50,000 - $74,999	27.6	34.7
$40,000 - $49,999	11.2	14.1
$30,000 - $39999	9.6	12.1
$20,000 - $29,999	7.2	9.0
$15,000 - $19,999	2.0	2.5
<$15,000yr	1.3	1.6

$2,638
$2,207
$1,886
$1,338
$949
$599
$331
$79

* Includes income tax health benefits exclusion (59%), Social
Security, OASDI and Medicare health insurance tax exclusions (32%),
out-of-pocket deductions and reimbursement accounts (8%).

FIGURE 2.3 Tax subsidies for employment-based insurance, by family income level, projected for 2000. NOTE: OASDI = Old age, survivors, and disability insurance.
SOURCE: Sheils et al., 1999, using Lewin Group estimates.

How People Gain Coverage	How People Lose Coverage
• Get a job where insurance is offered and premiums are affordable	• Lose a job where insurance was offered, so employer no longer subsidizes premiums
• Purchase insurance on your own, if you qualify and can afford the premiums	• Lose Medicaid or SCHIP eligibility once you or your children grow up or if your family's income increases
• Marry someone with insurance and if family out-of-pocket premiums are affordable	• Lose your spouse due to separation, divorce, or death
• Qualify for Medicaid, SCHIP, or Medicare	• Attain the age of 18 or graduate from college and lose eligibility under parents' plan
	• Your insurer goes out of business or cancels its contract with you, or your employer denies coverage to you
	• Be priced out of the market when the cost of premiums increases

FIGURE 2.4 Examples of ways in which people gain and lose health insurance. SOURCE: Adapted from Weissman and Epstein, 1994, Table 2-2.

Periods with No Coverage

For some people, lack of insurance is a temporary or one-time interruption of coverage, while for others, being uninsured is a periodically recurring experience or a permanent state of affairs. Brief, temporary lapses of health insurance coverage are less likely than longer uninsured periods to have significant detrimental effects on access to health care (Ayanian et al., 2000; Kasper et al., 2000). Yet even short periods with no insurance carry with them the financial risk of exposure to extraordinary health expenses. As a result, both the stability of insurance coverage and the length of uninsured periods have the potential to affect the health and financial well-being of individuals, families, and communities.

Longitudinal surveys provide the basis for estimating the prevalence and duration of uninsured spells. During 1994, the latest year for which the Survey of Income and Program Participation (SIPP) results are available, an estimated 53 million Americans, or 21 percent of the population under age 65, were uninsured for at least one month (Bennefield, 1998a). The median duration of periods without insurance is between 5 and 6 months, measured over a 36–month period. Those who are uninsured for less than six months are at some financial risk for incurring extraordinarily high medical expenses while uncovered, whereas those who are uninsured for longer periods face increased chances of problems in obtaining health care as well as experiencing cumulatively greater financial risks.

The duration and frequency of periods without insurance vary with the source of coverage and among different populations. One analysis of periods without coverage found family income, educational attainment and employment sector as measured just before the loss of health insurance to have the strongest effect on the length of time uninsured. The authors of this study concluded that policies to address the problem of uninsurance need to take into account the precipitating factors in losing and gaining coverage as well as the income, workplace and personal characteristics often associated with periods of uninsurance of varying lengths (Swartz et al., 1993a). Policy interventions need to be designed with an awareness of the populations and problems that they ultimately affect: either those who experience short periods without coverage or persons who remain uninsured for longer intervals. Often a single strategy does not address both kinds of problems (Short and Klerman, 1998).

People who previously had individual insurance account for more than half of all uninsured periods, perhaps because the cost of individual insurance is relatively high and may become unaffordable or because an insurance company refuses to renew a policy if the holder becomes a bad risk. Those who lose employment-based coverage account for only one-third of uninsured periods (Jensen, 1992). This is notable given that more than two-thirds of the public have employment-based coverage and only 7 percent have individual coverage. Young adults age 18–24, workers with job interruptions, and persons in lower-income families (less than 200 percent of FPL) all have roughly a 50 percent chance of going without health coverage for at least one month during a three year period (Bennefield, 1998a). Children, young adults, persons with some college education, and full-time workers tend to experience shorter periods uninsured than do adults who have not attended college or who work part-time, are unemployed, or are not in the labor force (Bennefield, 1998a).

Low-income uninsured persons tend to stay uninsured for longer than those with higher incomes. The typical or median time period without coverage for someone below the FPL is significantly longer than for all other persons—more than 8 months compared with 6 months (McBride, 1997).

Coverage is particularly episodic for lower income women. Medicaid enrollment periods for single women tend to be short; more than half maintain enrollment for less than one year, not quite one-third last more than two years, and only 15 percent last longer than five years. One study of a sample of unmarried women between the ages of 19 and 44 found that one-third of all new Medicaid enrollees had private health insurance just prior to enrolling in Medicaid (Short and Freedman, 1998). Among former welfare recipients who lost Medicaid benefits, one year after leaving welfare 28–38 percent had private coverage, 36–49 percent were uninsured, and 22–26 percent had returned to Medicaid (Garrett and Holahan, 2000; Short and Freedman, 1998).

CONSTRAINED COVERAGE OPTIONS

The substantial cost of health insurance means that employers and consumers alike face difficult choices about when and how much health insurance to purchase.

Difficult Choices for Employers

The cost and availability of group policies to employers reflects the gamut of insurance company practices, state regulations, and constraints imposed by ERISA and HIPAA, which prohibit employer discrimination in eligibility for coverage based on health status. The average cost of a family policy in an employment-based group was $6,351 per year in 2000 (Kaiser–HRET, 2000). The price for a particular insurance policy may be affected by insurance company practices ranging from risk-rating (based either on the group's experience or medical underwriting) to restrictions on coverage of specific persons, populations, conditions, or episodes. The price of the insurance premium offered to a firm reflects a number of considerations, including firm size, whether it is unionized, the employment sector, and federal tax policies. In addition, an insurance company may decline to offer or to renew a group policy at all, based on decisions related to underwriting practices. Group health insurance premiums vary geographically, with the highest individual and family coverage premiums occurring in the Northeast region, and the lowest in the West. This regional variation amounts to about 15 percentage points around the national average premium price (Kaiser–HRET, 2000).

Employers have used direct and indirect means to constrain their health insurance costs. Although the share of the health insurance premium paid directly by the employee varies from none to all, workers on average pay 14 percent of the cost of individual coverage and 27 percent of the cost of family coverage (Kaiser–HRET, 2000). From 1979 through 1995, when the cost of health services rose more quickly than did real income, one common employer response to price increases was to reduce the size and proportion of their subsidy of their employees' health insurance premiums, with lower-wage workers experiencing the greatest decline in subsidy (Medoff et al., 2001). For example, between 1988 and 1996, the proportion of the average worker's share for single coverage increased from 10 percent to 22 percent (GAO, 1997a). The proportion paid for family coverage increased more slowly, from 26 percent to 30 percent (and from 34 to 44 percent for coverage offered by small to medium-sized firms), although the dollar cost of the average worker's share for family coverage increased more than for single coverage, an 111 percent increase compared with a 79 percent increase for single coverage (Gabel et al., 1997; GAO, 1997a). Since 1996 the trend has been toward smaller proportional and absolute premium payments by employees for individual coverage and roughly steady employee contributions for family coverage (Kaiser–HRET, 2000). Also, fewer employers are extending coverage to retirees, who, if they retire before age 65, must find an individual policy to cover them until they become eligible for Medicare (McArdle et al., 1999; Fronstin, 2001; GAO, 2001b).

Small employers usually face higher group health insurance premium rates than do large employers. Larger firms can cushion themselves from the financial impact of insurance company underwriting practices and restrictions by choosing to self-insure their employee's health benefits, often using a third-party administrator. Small employers may receive poorer benefits for premiums comparable to those of large firms, because of both a higher risk premium and higher administrative costs per person. Insurers may decline to write policies, or write relatively expensive ones, for small to midsized firms in particular employment sectors such as seasonal workers or hazardous occupations (Weissman and Epstein, 1994). Because wage rates tend to be lower in smaller firms, the financial strain on both employers and workers is increased (Gabel, 1999). As a result, some small employers simply decline to offer coverage. Among small businesses surveyed, the most common and highest-ranking reason for not offering insurance benefits was the expense of coverage (Fronstin and Helman, 2000).

Difficult Choices for Individuals

Financial concerns constrain a person's decision to enroll in employment-sponsored coverage or to purchase individual health insurance. The choice the individual or family makes reflects the value decision makers place on avoiding risk, their beliefs or expectations about future health care needs and costs, the anticipated out-of-pocket costs (including any premiums and copayments), and the ability of the family to pay such costs. The choice reflects, in part, a comparison of employee premium costs and health care costs not covered by the policy, which constitute the individual's or family's out-of-pocket expenditures, with what they expect to incur in total health care costs, plus some allowance for the desire to avoid the risk of higher payments absent insurance. It also reflects the value of health services relative to other goods and services the family needs, such as food, rent, and utilities. Estimates of consumers' responsiveness to changes in the price of health insurance based on the choices of workers without employment-based coverage reveal that such purchase decisions are not very sensitive to price (Marquis and Long, 1995).[5]

The expense of the insurance premiums paid by employees tops the list of reasons why uninsured workers decline to take employment-based insurance when it is offered (Cooper and Schone, 1997). Between 1979 and 1995, the proportion of workers who paid less than 5 percent of their family income for health care expenditures (including expenses covered by private health insurance) declined by half, from about 50 percent to 26 percent, while the proportion of workers who paid over 10 percent of their family income increased by over half, from 20 percent to 33 percent (Kronick and Gilmer, 1999). A recent survey found that uninsured adults cite the expense of insurance as a major or the most important reason they do not have coverage (Hoffman and Schlobohm, 2000). Although almost 16 million Americans under the age of 65 purchase individual health

---

[5] The authors of this study estimate a price elasticity of −0.3 to −0.4 and an income elasticity of 0.15 using Current Population Survey and Survey of Income and Program Participation data from 1988 and 1987, respectively, and prices for a standard insurance product in different market areas.

insurance policies directly from insurers or their agents rather than through an employer, the higher cost of individual nongroup coverage limits its use, and persons in poor health may be excluded from this market altogether.

Often the offer of health insurance through the workplace entails significant premium costs that must be paid directly by the employee, particularly for family coverage (Figure 2.5). The average employer premium contribution of 86 percent for individual and 73 percent for family coverage conceals a highly variable set of arrangements (Kaiser–HRET, 2000). In firms with low-waged workers (i.e., more than a third of the work force earns less than $20,000 annually), employers contribute a smaller proportion of the premium. The lower level of employer contribution to family premiums in low-waged firms (63 percent compared to 73 percent overall) adds $53 per month on average to the employee's cost, above the national average of $138 monthly for family coverage (Kaiser–HRET, 2000). For a worker earning $20,000 per year, roughly $10 per hour, the employee's cost for family coverage would be more than 11 percent of before-tax income.

For all families, but particularly those of lower and moderate income and for persons faced with a health problem, cost considerations often limit choices. Families with very limited income may have to choose between paying a high share of family income on health insurance premiums or having to decline enroll-

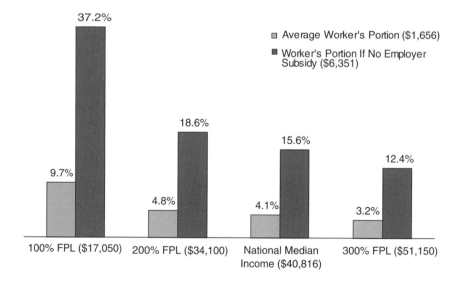

FIGURE 2.5 How much of a four-person family's yearly income would be needed to purchase an average employment-based health insurance premium for family coverage in 2000?
SOURCES: Kaiser–HRET 2000; U.S. Census Bureau, 2000; U.S. Department of Health and Human Services, 2000.

ment to be able to pay for rent, food, and other necessities. However, by declining enrollment, they risk a wide range of adverse impacts on health, family well-being, and financial stability.

Four out of five people without insurance (82 percent) are members of families in which at least one person works full- or part-time during the year (Hoffman and Pohl, 2000). Only 55 percent of workers whose hourly rate is below $7 are offered employment-based insurance, through either their own or a family member's job, compared with 96 percent of workers whose hourly rate is above $15. The proportion of employees who choose to enroll in their employment-based plan or a family member's health plan when given the opportunity is 76 percent for the lowest wage workers, compared with 94 percent for the highest-wage workers (Cooper and Schone, 1997).

INSURANCE TRENDS

For both children and adults, the number without health insurance and their relative proportion of the total population grew through the recessions of the late 1970s, the mid-1980s, and the early 1990s, as well as during the periods of economic prosperity in between and since the mid-1990s (Holahan and Kim, 2000). The numbers of the uninsured have increased by almost a third since 1987 when an estimated 32 million people under age 65 were uninsured, while their share of the overall population has grown more slowly, from 15 percent in 1987 to 17.5 percent in 1999 (Fronstin, 2000d).

Since the latter part of the 1970s, the prime economic force behind the rising numbers of uninsured Americans, and the declining proportion of Americans covered through employment-based insurance, has been the gap created as the rise in real income or purchasing power has lagged behind increases in health services costs and the costs involved in purchasing health insurance (Figure 2.6) (Cooper and Schone, 1997; Holahan and Kim, 2000). In constant 1998 dollars, the cost of employment-based health insurance increased 250 percent between 1977 and 1998 and the employee's share of insurance premiums increased 350 percent (Gabel, 1999). During that same period, median household incomes increased in real terms by 17 percent (U.S. Census Bureau, 2000). After having stabilized as a percentage of the Gross Domestic Product (GDP) between 1993 and 1999, health care spending is once again projected to increase over the next ten years in relation to GDP (Heffler et al., 2001). Health insurance premiums increased faster in 1999 than in the previous five-year period (6.5 percent compared with a 5 percent average annual growth rate) (Heffler et al., 2001).

Declines in Employment-Based Coverage

Counter to the long-term trend, employment-based health insurance has been growing since 1994 and contributed to a small reduction in the national uninsured rate for the first time in 1999. This reduction in the likelihood of being

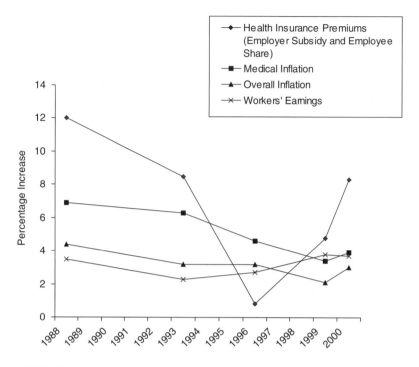

FIGURE 2.6 Health insurance premiums increased more quickly than earnings, 1988–1999.
SOURCE: Kaiser–HRET, 2000.

uninsured has occurred within the context of a robust economy over the preceding six years. Over the longer term (since the late 1970s) there has been a decline in employment-based coverage. Between 1979 and 1997, health insurance coverage rates for government workers and their families remained relatively stable at about 80 percent, while coverage of workers employed in the private sector and their families declined by 7 percentage points to 64 percent (Farber and Levy, 2000). Two factors contributed to this decline in private-sector employment-based coverage. First, eligibility for employment-based insurance decreased for "peripheral" workers (those in part-time or recently acquired positions). Second, the take-up rate for "core" workers (those who have held full-time positions for a longer period) declined (Farber and Levy, 2000). This gradual but extended decline in employment-based coverage appears to have ended after reaching a low of 64 percent in 1993 (Fronstin, 2000d).[6]

---

[6]Because of changes in the Current Population Survey questionnaire and sampling procedures beginning with the March 1995 survey, most analysts caution against overinterpreting changes during the 1993–1994 period (Holahan and Kim, 2000).

Through the early 1990s, declines in employment-based coverage were partially attenuated by modest growth in public insurance and individually purchased coverage. Increases in the uninsured rate since the mid-1990s have been attributed to declines in public insurance and individually purchased coverage, despite increases since 1993 in employment-based coverage (Holahan and Kim, 2000).

Ups and Downs in Public Program Enrollment

Fundamental changes in public policies have affected both the size and the composition of the uninsured population over the last 15 years. Expansions of Medicaid eligibility for children and pregnant women beginning in the mid-1980s boosted eligibility and, to a lesser degree, enrollments in state public insurance programs. In the mid-1990s, enrollment in public insurance decreased sharply with the enactment of the Personal Responsibility and Work Opportunities Reconciliation Act of 1996 (PRWORA), which uncoupled Medicaid eligibility from income support and placed new restrictions on legal immigrants' eligibility, including a five-year bar on participation by immigrants arriving after August 1996 (Ku and Blaney, 2000; Rosenbaum, 2000; Guendelman et al., 2001; Holahan et al., 2001; Ku and Matani, 2001).[7] Many lower-income parents (mostly women) did not enroll because they either lost eligibility for Medicaid or believed that they were no longer eligible because of their loss of income benefits (Garrett and Holahan, 2000; Holahan, 2001). Although the PRWORA's provisions were intended to allow families to maintain health coverage after cash benefits ended, separate enrollment processes for the two programs and confusion have contributed to reduced Medicaid enrollments.

Since the implementation of SCHIP, there has been some recovery of public coverage for lower-income children. However, an estimated 94 percent of uninsured children in lower-income families are eligible for public insurance but not fully enrolled: all but 400,000 of the estimated 7.1 million uninsured lower-income children (Broaddus and Ku, 2000). SCHIP has experienced slow growth in its first years, and serious problems remain in reaching enrollment targets. While 3.3 million children had been enrolled by October 2000, maintaining children's participation in SCHIP beyond the first enrollment period presents additional challenges (Broaddus and Ku, 2000; Cunningham and Park, 2000).

Prospects for Employment-Based Coverage

A continuation of the economic slowdown that began in late 2000, or a further softening of the labor market, could erase the modest gains made in employment-based coverage since 1994 (GAO, 2001a). A recent study by the

---

[7]States have the option to cover legal immigrants arriving before August 1996 and the option to cover them after the five-year period.

Center for Risk Management and Insurance Research at Georgia State University suggests that a strong economy and competitive labor market do affect employment-based coverage rates. This analysis identified a rising wage level as accounting for more than half of the observed increase in employment-based coverage between 1997 and 1999 (Custer and Ketsche, 2000a). When the authors of this study projected the current estimate of 42 million uninsured Americans eight years forward, based on different economic scenarios, they concluded (Custer and Ketsche, 2000a):

- "Assuming continued economic growth and moderate health care cost inflation, the number of uninsured Americans will rise to more than 48 million in 2009.
- In the event of a recession, the number who lack coverage will reach 61 million by 2009.
- Rapid economic growth coupled with rapid health care cost inflation, such as characterized the 1980s, would lead to roughly 55 million uninsured in 2009."

Under a different and more optimistic scenario, even if the most recent rate of decline in the number of uninsured Americans continues for five more years, an estimated 34 million people would still be uninsured by 2005 (Fronstin, 2001).

According to U.S. Labor Department unemployment filings, mass layoffs (50 or more workers) lasting more than 30 days increased by 25 percent, comparing the first calendar quarter of 2001 with the first quarter of 2000. Manufacturing industries accounted for an increasing share of all layoffs (U.S. Department of Labor, 2001). The manufacturing sector is one that is more likely to offer health benefits, which workers who are laid off may lose if they cannot afford to pay the premiums.

SUMMARY

This chapter has described the conditions under which health insurance coverage is obtained and lost, and the individual, economic and policy factors that affect opportunities for coverage and that increase or diminish the likelihood of being uninsured. The following chapter presents a detailed picture of that cross-section of Americans who are uninsured and the relative burdens of uninsurance among various population groups.

NOTES

Box 3.1

People may lack coverage regardless of education, age, or state of residence. Employment and geographic factors are central because private insurance is closely tied to employment and eligibility for public programs is partly determined by work and income criteria.

- Full-time, full-year employment offers families the best chances of having health insurance, as does an annual income of at least a moderate level (greater than 200 percent of the federal poverty level, or FPL). Two-thirds of all uninsured persons are members of families who earn less than 200 percent of FPL, and nearly one-third of all members of lower-income families are uninsured.
- The average person's chances of being uninsured rise and then fall over the course of a lifetime. Children have a lower-than-average chance of being uninsured, young adults a higher-than-average likelihood, and middle-age and older adults face a gradually diminishing likelihood of lacking coverage. Because of Medicare, persons over age 65 are rarely uninsured.
- Just over half of all uninsured persons are non-Hispanic whites. Higher-than-average uninsured rates among racial and ethnic minority groups and among recent immigrants reflect lower rates of employment-based coverage and lower family incomes, on average, compared to non-Hispanic whites and U.S.-born residents. African Americans are twice as likely as non-Hispanic whites to be uninsured, and Hispanics are three times as likely to be uninsured. Foreign-born residents are almost three times as likely as persons born in the United States to be uninsured and, among the foreign born, non-citizens are more than twice as likely as citizens to be uninsured.
- Gender disparities in coverage reflect the different experiences of adult men and women in the workplace and public policies. Although men are more likely than women to lack coverage, women have a lower rate of employment-based coverage. Because women are more likely to obtain coverage through individual policies and public programs, their insurance status tends to be less stable, with more opportunities for gaps in coverage.
- Differences in population characteristics, industrial economic base, eligibility for public insurance, and the relative purchasing power of family incomes shape geographic disparities in insurance coverage rates. Residents of the South and West are more likely than average to be uninsured. Most uninsured persons live in urban areas, although rural and urban residents are about equally likely to be uninsured.

3

Who Goes Without Health Insurance? Who Is Most Likely to Be Uninsured?

This chapter provides a portrait of the uninsured, to support the Committee's future reports about the consequences of uninsurance. Here, the Committee reviews and summarizes the published literature about what socioeconomic, demographic, and geographic characteristics describe the uninsured both collectively and as members of groups in the general population that are more likely than average to be uninsured.[1] Supporting methodological information and data tables provide the numbers behind the general statements in the text and can be found in Appendixes C and D. All estimates are for persons uninsured during calendar year 1999 (the most recent available Current Population Survey data), unless otherwise indicated.

The large number and variety of Americans who are uninsured underscore the Committee's conclusion that the voluntary, employment-based approach to insurance coverage in the United States functions less like a system and more like a sieve. There are many ways to slip through the holes. People of all ages, levels of education, and in all states may be uninsured, although socioeconomic and geo-

---

[1]There is a wealth of information about the characteristics of uninsured persons, families, and populations. In addition to the public surveys and databases conducted and maintained by federal agencies such as the Bureau of the Census and the Department of Health and Human Services, surveys and studies of insurance coverage and uninsured persons are supported by the Employee Benefit Research Institute, the Commonwealth Fund, the Kaiser Commission on Medicaid and the Uninsured, the Urban Institute's Assessing the New Federalism project, and The Robert Wood Johnson Foundation through the Community Tracking Study conducted by the Center for Studying Health System Change.

graphic factors that affect coverage are highly correlated. One's chances of being uninsured increase if one works in an occupation or in an employment sector where employers are less likely to offer a health benefit, if one is self-employed or works for a small private-sector firm, or if one has too low an income to afford coverage.

The final section of this chapter includes estimates of the relative importance of key social, economic, demographic, and geographic characteristics to one's likelihood of being uninsured, based on a new multivariate analysis of published data. Most of the studies that the Committee reviewed are based on two-way (bivariate) analyses of a characteristic and the probability that an individual with that characteristic will be uninsured.

Throughout the chapter, the Committee addresses two questions together:

1. What are the characteristics of the uninsured population?
2. Who is most likely to be uninsured?

The distribution of socioeconomic, demographic, and geographic differences in the general population under age 65 affects how these characteristics are distributed among the uninsured population because the relative size of specific population groups affects their representation among the uninsured. For example, the uninsured *rate* for the urban population is the same as that of the rural population, although four out of five uninsured people live in urban areas, reflecting the predominance of urban populations nationally.

HOW SOCIAL AND ECONOMIC FACTORS AFFECT COVERAGE

Full-time, full-year employment offers families the best chances of acquiring and keeping health insurance, as does an annual income of at least a moderate level (greater than 200 percent of the federal poverty level [FPL]). Insured status correlates highly with many aspects of employment, including work status, income level, educational attainment, occupation, and employer characteristics such as firm size and employment sector.

Work Status

Eight out of every ten uninsured people are members of families with at least one wage earner, and six out of every ten uninsured people are wage earners themselves. Nonetheless, members of families without wage earners are much more likely to be uninsured than members of families with wage earners.

Families with at least one full-time, full-year worker are more than twice as likely to have health insurance coverage, compared to families whose wage earners work part-time (less than 35 hours per week), as contingent labor (e.g., on a seasonal or temporary basis, as employees of contractors, self-employed), or in which there is no wage earner (Copeland et al., 1999; Hoffman and Pohl, 2000; Thorpe and Florence, 1999) (Figures 3.1 and 3.2). The availability of health insurance in the workplace is the most important factor in determining whether wage earners and their families are insured. Yet more than half of the uninsured under age 65 years are members of families with one full-time, full-year worker. Fully 82 percent of uninsured persons are members of families with at least one wage earner (Hoffman and Pohl, 2000).

As discussed in Chapter 2, the rate of employment-based coverage has declined since the late 1970s, with wage earners in long-term, full-time positions ("core jobs") more likely to be insured than persons recently employed or working less than full-time ("peripheral jobs") (Farber and Levy, 2000). Contingent workers are less likely than full-time, permanent workers to be offered employment-based coverage and less likely to take up or enroll in an offered plan, although they may receive insurance through a spouse (Buchmueller, 1996–1997; Copeland et al., 1999). Given the relatively small proportion of contingent workers in the labor market (an estimated 10 percent in 1995) and the uniform decline in coverage rates among employment sectors during the 1980s, the net decline in employment-based coverage appears to have been driven by changes other than an increasing number of contingent workers (Long and Rodgers, 1995; Copeland et al., 1999). However, ongoing and future labor force changes may have more of an adverse impact on employment-based coverage rates. One study has predicted that greater numbers of part-time workers may cause the employment-based

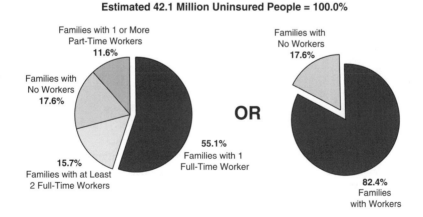

Estimated 42.1 Million Uninsured People = 100.0%

FIGURE 3.1 Distribution of uninsured population under age 65, by work status of self or family breadwinner, 1999. NOTE: Numbers may not add to 100.0 percent due to rounding.
SOURCE: Hoffman and Pohl, 2000.

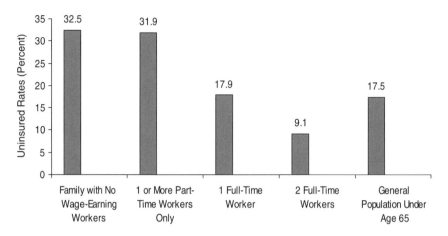

FIGURE 3.2 Probability of being uninsured for the population under age 65, by work status of self or of primary wage earner, 1999.
SOURCE: Hoffman and Pohl, 2000.

coverage rate to decline by 1 to 7 percentage points by the year 2008 (Acs and Blumberg, 2001).

Most uninsured wage earners are lower income (earning less than 200 percent of FPL) or moderate income (between 200 and 400 percent of FPL) (Budetti et al., 1999; Fronstin, 2000d; O'Brien and Feder, 1998). Members of lower-income wage-earning families are more likely to lack coverage than are members of moderate- and higher-income families. This is a function of both the reduced likelihood that lower-waged jobs offer health benefits and the relatively costly premium, compared to income, paid by lower-income families to purchase employment-based coverage (Gabel et al., 1999; O'Brien and Feder, 1999).

Income and Poverty

Two-thirds of all uninsured persons are members of lower-income families (earning less than 200 percent of FPL). One-third of all members of lower-income families are uninsured.

There are uninsured people at all income levels, although members of families earning less than 200 percent of FPL are twice as likely to be uninsured as are members of the general population under age 65 (Fronstin, 2000d).[2] Translating

---

[2] In this discussion the term "family" is used to describe both a kinship and an economic relationship (e.g., a single adult is considered to be a one-person family). Family income levels are defined as follows:

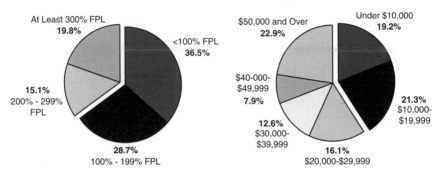

FIGURE 3.3 Distribution of uninsured population under age 65, by family income level, 1999. NOTE: Numbers may not add to 100.0 percent due to rounding. SOURCE: Fronstin, 2000d.

percentages of the FPL into dollars allows for a more vivid comparison: almost two of ten uninsured persons are members of families that earn less than $10,000 per year (Fronstin, 2000d). A family of four must have an income greater than 400 percent of FPL (for 1999, $66,800) to have less than a one in ten chance of being uninsured (Figures 3.3 and 3.4) (Custer and Ketsche, 2000b).

Higher income does not necessarily mean a lower uninsured rate. Eligibility for most public insurance (means-tested categorical programs) is restricted to specific categories of low- and lower-income persons. Many members of lower-income families are not eligible for public insurance, yet they are not offered—nor can they afford to buy—employment-based or individual health insurance. In addition, the number and relative sizes of salaries that make up a family's income may determine whether employment-based health insurance is offered at all. A family having a single wage earner with a salary of $50,000 is more likely to have

---

• Low income: an annual income of less than 100 percent of the FPL, which is established on a yearly basis for different types of family groups that comprise a given household, for example, one adult, or one adult and two children;

• lower income: an annual income less than 200 percent of FPL; and

• moderate income: an annual income between 200 and 400 percent of FPL for a given family group.

Table C.1 (Appendix C) lists incomes at the FPL and multiples of the FPL for individuals and families of different sizes. In 1999, 200 percent of the FPL for one person was an annual income of $16,480, for a family of two, $22,120, and for a family of 3, $27,760.

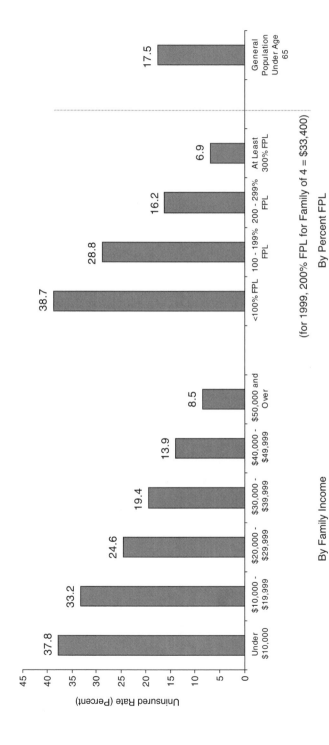

FIGURE 3.4 Probability of being uninsured for population under age 65, by income and poverty level, 1999. SOURCE: Hoffman and Pohl, 2000.

access to health insurance than is a family with two wage earners, each of whom earns an annual salary of $25,000.[3]

Federal policies have expanded the income eligibility standards for public insurance for specific categories of lower-income persons. However, only some states have adopted these higher standards. Few states offer enrollment to children in families earning more than 200 percent of FPL or to adults in families earning at least 100 percent of FPL. For this reason, persons from families with earnings between 100 and 199 percent of FPL are almost as likely to go without coverage as are people from families whose earnings are below 100 percent of FPL (Hoffman and Schlobohm, 2000). Expansions of the Medicaid program from the mid-1980s through the mid-1990s and the introduction of the State Children's Insurance Programs (SCHIP) helped reduce the proportion of lower-income persons without health insurance from an estimated 38 percent in 1987 to an estimated 32 percent in 1999. These expansions left unchanged the principle that nondisabled persons ages 18–64 may be eligible for Medicaid only when they are parents living in households with children.

Educational Attainment

More than one-quarter of all uninsured adults have not earned a high school diploma. Almost four of every ten adults who have not graduated from high school are uninsured.

Employment-based health insurance coverage is associated increasingly with the presence of a college degree (Figures 3.5 and 3.6) (Gabel, 1999). In addition to being positively related to income, the attainment of a college degree is associated with employment in certain sectors and types of jobs that are more likely than others to include a health insurance benefit. Also, the worker's educational level has a small effect on the take-up rate of insurance offers. The decline in employment-based coverage between 1977 and 1998 almost entirely affected primary wage earners who had not graduated from college and their dependents (Gabel, 1999). Compared with a relatively steady 80 percent employment-based coverage rate for college graduates, high school graduates experienced a 5 percentage point decline in employment-based coverage (from 68 percent to 63 percent insured) between 1977 and 1998. Primary wage earners who did not complete high school experienced an 18 percentage point decline in employment-based coverage rate (from 52 percent to 34 percent) during this same time period. Years of education serve to protect against the loss of insurance for holders of core jobs but not for contingent or recently hired workers (Farber and Levy, 2000).

This pattern is influenced by both labor force and employer characteristics— for example an employer's willingness to offer a health benefit with affordable premiums or a subsidy. Almost seven out of ten workers (69 percent) without a

[3]This may reflect greater subsidy for higher-waged positions (Morrisey, 1993; Blumberg, 1999).

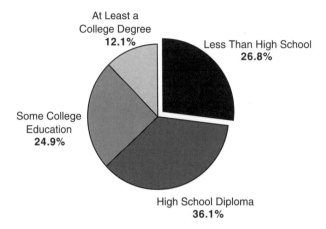

Estimated 31.3 Million Uninsured Adults = 100.0%

FIGURE 3.5 Distribution of uninsured adults (ages 19–64 years), by level of educational attainment, 1999. NOTE: Numbers may not add to 100.0 percent due to rounding. SOURCE: Hoffman and Pohl, 2000.

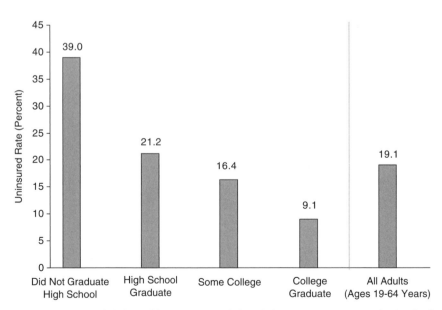

FIGURE 3.6 Probability of being uninsured for adults (ages 19–64 years), by level of educational attainment, 1999.
SOURCE: Hoffman and Pohl, 2000.

high school diploma are offered employment-based coverage. The take-up rate for this group of workers is 82 percent, only modestly below the overall worker take-up rate of 85 percent. Of those with high school diplomas or less education who are offered and decline coverage however, more than a third (36 percent) remain uninsured, twice the rate of residual uninsurance as that of more highly educated workers who decline workplace coverage. Less educated workers who decline coverage are less likely to gain coverage through a spouse than are more educated workers who decline coverage (Custer and Ketsche, 2000b). The decline in employment-based coverage of primary wage earners with less education may be attributed to the expense of coverage, whereas workers with higher educational attainment may have other options for coverage.

Job Characteristics

There are greater numbers of uninsured blue-collar workers than uninsured white-collar workers. Members of families with a primary wage earner who is blue collar are more likely to be uninsured than are members of families with a white-collar worker.

In addition to the job characteristics related to work status, the occupation of a family's primary wage earner influences the likelihood that members will be uninsured (McDonnell and Fronstin, 1999). Uninsured rates vary dramatically with regard to occupation: while almost half of all wage-earners working in private households (maids and domestic laborers) are uninsured, less than 10 percent of all wage earners in professional jobs are uninsured (McDonnell and Fronstin, 1999).

Employer Characteristics

Wage-earners in smaller-sized firms, in lower-waged firms, in non-unionized firms, and in nonmanufacturing employment sectors are more likely to go without coverage.

Over the past decade, the overall increase in the number of uninsured persons in working families has reflected a variety of dynamics related to employment-based coverage. There are greater numbers of uninsured workers employed by smaller firms (fewer than 25 employees), compared to larger firms, more employed in predominantly lower-waged or nonunionized firms, and more employed in sales ("wholesale and retail trade") compared to the profile of employers and industries that dominated the U.S. economy in the years after World War II when our present employment-based coverage arrangements became established (Gabel, 1999; Starr, 1982).

Economies of scale for employers in purchasing health benefit plans—that is, lower costs per person for larger groups—mean that firm size plays a key role in influencing the availability of employment-based coverage (Fronstin, 2000d;

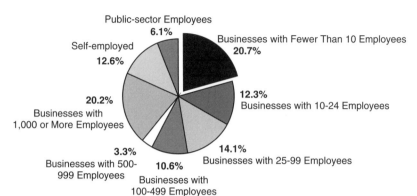

Estimated 24.2 Million Uninsured Wage Earners = 100.0%

FIGURE 3.7 Distribution of uninsured wage earners (ages 18–64 years), by size of employer's firm, 1999. NOTE: Numbers may not add to 100.0 percent due to rounding. SOURCE: Fronstin, 2000d.

Fronstin and Helman, 2000).[4] Of the six out of every ten uninsured persons who are wage earners, 46 percent are self-employed or work for private-sector firms with fewer than 25 employees; the uninsured rate for this subgroup is 28 percent (Figures 3.7 and 3.8) (Fronstin, 2000d). Firms that have at least 100 employees account for more than one-third of all uninsured workers, reflecting the fact that over 30 percent of the workforce is employed by larger firms. The uninsured rate for wage earners in medium- and larger-sized firms ranges between 12 and 16 percent (Fronstin, 2000d).

Greater numbers of uninsured workers and dependents exist where the workers are employed by lower-waged, compared to higher-waged firms, and by nonunion firms, compared to union firms (Fronstin, 2000d; Gabel et al., 1999; McDonnell and Fronstin, 1999). The chance of being uninsured is substantially greater for workers in small- to medium-sized firms (fewer than 200 employees) than for workers in larger firms (Kaiser–HRET, 2000). When more than one-third of these smaller firms' workers are considered lower-waged (earning less than $20,000 annually), the coverage rate by employers drops to about half (35 percent) of the coverage rate of comparable firms (85 percent) where less than one-third of workers are lower-waged (Kaiser–HRET, 2000). Since lower-waged workers are more likely to work for smaller firms, this contributes to a sizable disparity between the 43 percent offer rate for lower-waged workers (defined as earning $7 or

---

[4]The administrative costs of coverage per capita decrease with the increasing size of the employer's group.

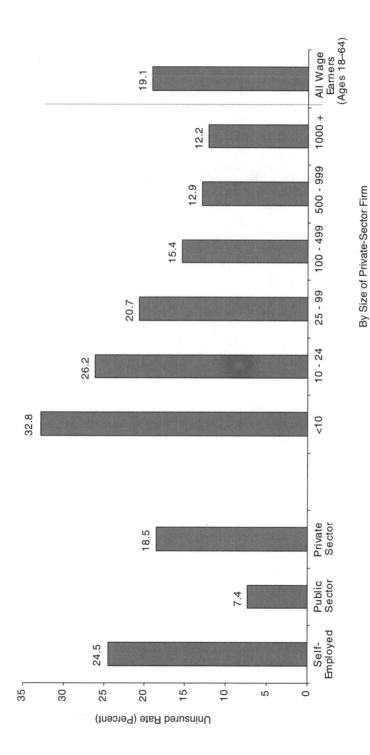

FIGURE 3.8 Probability of being uninsured for wage earners (ages 18–64 years), by size of employer's firm, 1999.
SOURCE: Fronstin, 2000d.

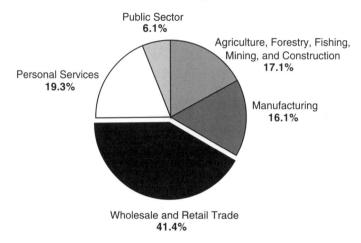

FIGURE 3.9 Distribution of uninsured wage earners (ages 18–64 years), by sector, 1999. NOTE: Numbers may not add to 100.0 percent due to rounding. SOURCE: Fronstin, 2000d.

less per hour) and the 93 percent offer rate for higher-waged workers (defined as earning more than $15 per hour) (Cooper and Schone, 1997, data for 1996).

The employment sector, such as manufacturing, agriculture or sales, also influences the probability that wage earners and their families will be uninsured (Figures 3.9 and 3.10). Members of families whose primary wage earners work in sales (wholesale and retail trade) comprise the single largest group of uninsured members of working families, more than four out of ten uninsured people (Fronstin, 2000b). Members of families whose primary wage earner works in sales are also more likely than the general population to be uninsured (22 percent uninsured rate). However, the highest uninsured rate is found among members of families whose primary wage earner works in employment sectors such as agriculture, forestry, fishing, mining, and construction. Almost one-third of all workers in this sector are uninsured (Fronstin, 2000d).

HOW COVERAGE VARIES OVER A PERSON'S LIFE

The average individual's chance of being uninsured traces an increasing and then decreasing path across his or her life span. This begins with a lower-than-average likelihood for children, a higher-than-average likelihood for young adults, followed by a gradual decline in the probability of being uninsured with advancing age and increasing connection to the labor force. At age 65, one

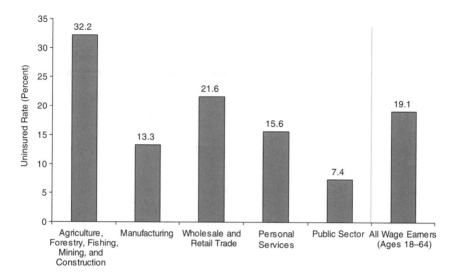

FIGURE 3.10 Probability of being uninsured for wage earners (ages 18-64 years), by sector, 1999.
SOURCE: Fronstin, 2000d.

has a minimal likelihood of being uninsured because Medicare provides nearly universal coverage. Marriage and the rearing of infants and young children both lower the chances, on average, that an adult will be uninsured. Within this broader trend, however, variations in sources of coverage and health status across age cohorts, as well as participation in the labor market, result in important differences.

Age

Three-quarters of the uninsured are adults (ages 18–64 years), while one-quarter of the uninsured are children. Compared with other age groups, young adults are the most likely to go without coverage.

The age distribution of uninsured persons relative to the total population reflects the availability of public programs for children and the decreasing number of uninsured adults in a specific age group as the group grows older. One-quarter of uninsured adults are between the ages of 18 and 24 years; more than one-quarter are between 25 and 34 years old; slightly less than a quarter are between 35 and 44 years; the remaining quarter of uninsured adults is comprised of persons between the ages of 45 and 64 (Figure 3.11) (Fronstin, 2000d). The age distribution of children without health insurance coverage is similar to the age distribution of children in the general population.

An estimated one out of every seven children (ages 0–17 years) is uninsured, while almost one out of every five adults (ages 18–64 years) is uninsured (Fronstin,

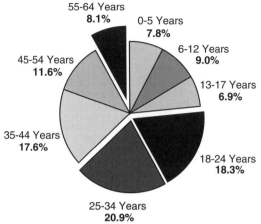

FIGURE 3.11 Distribution of uninsured population under age 65, by age group, 1999.
NOTE: Numbers may not add to 100.0 percent due to rounding.
SOURCE: Fronstin, 2000d.

2000d). Two groups of adults are of particular concern, young adults (ages 18 through 24 years) because of their high uninsured rate (29 percent) and midlife adults (ages 55 through 64 years) whose uninsured rate is lower than average (14 percent) but whose family incomes have begun to decline, on average, and who have a greater anticipated need for health services (Figure 3.12).

Young Adults (Ages 18 Through 24 Years)

Almost three out of every ten young adults do not have health insurance. Members of this age group are nearly twice as likely to be uninsured compared to members of the general population under age 65. This higher-than-average probability has been the case since at least the mid-1980s, and the uninsured rate for this group continues to increase over time (Rowland et al., 1998; Swartz, 1998; Quinn et al., 2000).

Overrepresentation of young adults among the uninsured reflects social, economic, and demographic factors. Young adulthood is a period of transition from school to work, likely to involve changes that may lead to gaps in health insurance coverage. For young adults who are not wage earners, family income is a key factor affecting their likelihood of being uninsured. Families covered by employment-based health insurance often extend coverage to children who are supported as full-time college students (usually through age 23). A family's ability to support one or more children as full-time college students usually reflects moderate or higher income levels. Even among full-time college students (6.5 million people),

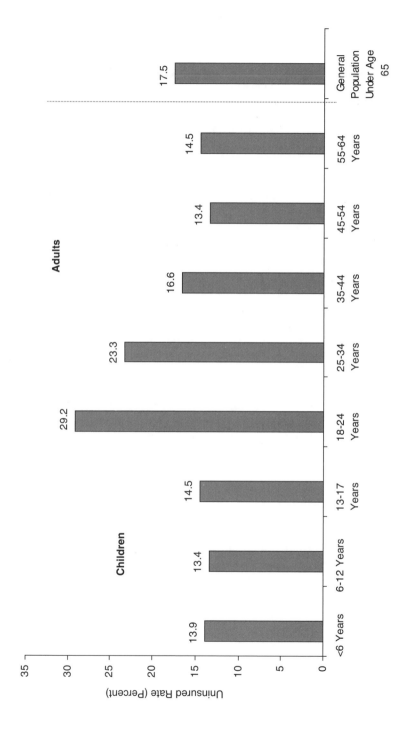

FIGURE 3.12 Probability of being uninsured for population under age 65, by age group, 1999.
SOURCE: Fronstin, 2000d.

the uninsured rate is relatively high—one out of every five students (about 1.3 million people). Of the remaining 12 million young adults who are not full-time college students, almost two out of five persons are uninsured (Quinn et al., 2000).

Social and economic factors present potential barriers to young adults trying to obtain coverage through employment-based plans. They are more likely to work in smaller firms, more likely to hold entry-level or lower-waged jobs (less than $10 per hour), and as a result, less likely to receive an offer of employment-based coverage (Custer and Ketsche, 2000b; Quinn et al., 2000). When health insurance is offered to young employees, it is more likely to require that the employee pay a relatively high proportion of the costs. Take-up rates for young adults are lower than for the adult population overall, although estimates of the difference vary with the data source and age ranges being compared (Cunningham, 1999a; McDonnell and Fronstin, 1999; Custer and Ketsche, 2000b). Nonetheless, young adults do share the views of older adults that health insurance is important, and they cite the cost of premiums as the most important reason for deciding not to enroll in a health plan (Quinn et al., 2000). Some young people, likely those with no option to buy coverage at work, buy individual coverage. One measure of the value of coverage is the fact that this age group shows a higher-than-average rate for individually purchased coverage (Figure 3.13) (Fronstin, 2000d).

Midlife Adults (Ages 55 Through 64 Years)

Midlife adults are less likely to go without health insurance than are members of the population overall, yet their risk is of particular concern because of their collective decline in income; their transition in work status from full-time, full-year work to contingent labor or retirement; and their decline in health status, accompanied by increased spending for health services (GAO, 1998; Brennan, 2000). During 1996, about one-third of midlife adults with family incomes under $10,000 were uninsured. For this age group, the uninsured rate dropped to less than 10 percent only for those whose family income was at least $40,000.

Adults between the ages of 55 and 64 are "the largest and most easily identifiable segment of the [medically] high-risk population," accounting for two-thirds of all deaths and more than one-third of all surgical procedures and hospital days among all adults under 65 years of age (Jensen, 1992). This is the age group most likely to report fair or poor health status, the presence of chronic disease, or the presence of a limiting condition or disability (Jensen, 1992; Brennan, 2000). In this age group, women are more likely than men to be uninsured and to suffer worse health (Monheit et al., 2001).

Given this age group's overall health status, the proportion of persons uninsured would be even higher than observed were it not for higher-than-average rates of enrollment in Medicaid and Medicare by the disabled and higher enrollment in individual insurance (GAO, 1998; Brennan, 2000). While uninsured midlife adults are more likely than other adults to purchase individual policies,

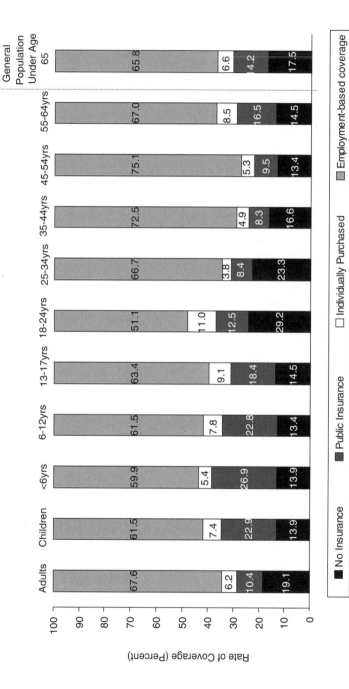

FIGURE 3.13 Sources of health insurance for population under 65 years, by age group, 1999. NOTE: Numbers may not add to 100.0 percent due to respondents reporting more than one source of coverage and due to rounding. SOURCE: Fronstin, 2000d.

they are also more likely to find these policies unaffordable (due to medical underwriting for individuals and experience rating for the age group), inadequate (e.g., preexisting conditions may be excluded from coverage), or unavailable (GAO, 1998). Men are significantly more likely to be covered by employment-based insurance and Medicare (when certified as being permanently disabled or as having end-stage renal disease), while women are significantly more likely to be covered by individual policies and by Medicaid (Brennan, 2000). Women's lower incomes contribute to greater Medicaid eligibility (Wyn et al., 2001).

Widening gaps in employment-based retiree health coverage mirror the overall decline in employment-based coverage. Over the past decade, there has been a decline in the number of large firms offering health insurance coverage to retirees (Fronstin, 2001). A December 1990 change in standard accounting practice (Federal Accounting Standard 106) has made explicit and transparent to investors the large unfunded liabilities inherent in employers' promises of retiree benefits, discouraging employers from offering a health insurance benefit to new retirees (GAO, 1998; Fronstin, 2001). Wage-earners who retire before age 65 because of a health condition may find themselves uninsured if their employer does not offer retiree coverage, if the cost to continue enrollment in the employer's plan is prohibitive, or if individual insurance coverage is too costly or not available.

Children

Federal and state policies have given high priority to providing health insurance opportunities for children, yet the uninsured rate for children is almost 14 percent and an estimated two-thirds of all uninsured children are believed to be eligible for public insurance (Broaddus and Ku, 2000; Mills, 2000).

Between 1977 and 1996, the uninsured rate for children rose, consistent with the decline in employment-based coverage for adults over the same period (Weinick and Monheit, 1999). From 1994 through 1998, half of the increase in the number of uninsured children consisted of children from lower-income families (less than 200 percent of FPL) and the other half from families with at least a moderate income level (at least 200 percent of FPL) (Holahan and Kim, 2000). Between 1998 and 1999, when the coverage rate improved for the first time in more than a decade, children accounted for 60 percent (1 million people) of the overall decline in the total number of uninsured people (Guyer, 2000).

Since 1995 there has been a decline in the proportion of children covered by Medicaid, reflecting the impact of the 1996 welfare reform that uncoupled Medicaid eligibility and enrollment from public income assistance (Broaddus and Ku, 2000). Independent of the economic prosperity that began in the mid-1990s, welfare reform is estimated to have caused a decline in public health insurance coverage of between 8 and 13 percentage points for children from low-income families (less than 100 percent of FPL) (Guyer, 2000; Kronebusch, 2001).

Some of the losses in Medicaid coverage for children from lower-income families have been recouped by SCHIP (Guyer, 2000). Medicaid now covers one in four children overall. Nonetheless almost all lower-income uninsured children (7 million) are eligible for either Medicaid or SCHIP (Broaddus and Ku, 2000). There are continuing problems with program outreach, enrollment, and maintenance of enrollment (Broaddus and Ku, 2000; Cunningham and Park, 2000). By 2002, all low-income children (family income less than 100 percent of FPL) should be eligible for public insurance under either Medicaid or SCHIP (Broaddus and Ku, 2000). It is anticipated that SCHIP will reduce the proportion of children who are uninsured as states more fully implement their programs and if current funding streams are maintained or expanded (Selden et al., 1999).

Marital Status

There are more unmarried than married adults among the ranks of the uninsured. Unmarried persons are much more likely than are those who are married to be uninsured.

Marriage often serves as a protective factor against being uninsured; 29 percent of uninsured adults are married, while 35 percent of uninsured adults report themselves as never having been married and 11 percent report themselves as being divorced (Rhoades and Chu, 2000). If both spouses in a married couple are wage earners, they have two potential chances to obtain coverage, through one spouse's employer or the other's. Furthermore, the family income of married couples, like that of two-parent families, may reflect the contribution of more than one wage-earner, giving a potential economic advantage in comparison with the family incomes of single people and single parents. As a result, married couples may be more likely to find that health insurance premiums are affordable (Figure 3.14). The uninsured rate for two single adults living together (35 percent) is higher than the uninsured rate either for single adults living alone (16 percent) or for married adults without children (17 percent) (Hoffman and Schlobohm, 2000).

Young adults are less likely to be married and, thus, less likely to have the chance to obtain coverage through a spouse. Only 15 percent of young adults ages 19 to 23 years are married and 3 percent are covered by their spouse (Quinn et al., 2000). For people aged 24 to 29 years, almost half are married and 11 percent receive insurance coverage through a spouse, compared to those ages 30 to 64, of whom two-thirds are married and 18 percent are covered by a spouse's policy.

Family Composition

More than half of all uninsured persons are members of families that include children, and more than half of all uninsured children live in two-parent families, comparable to their numbers in the general population. However, individuals in families without children are more likely to go without coverage than those in families that include children.

The fact that families with children are more likely to be insured may reflect the slower rate of increase in insurance premium costs over time for employment-

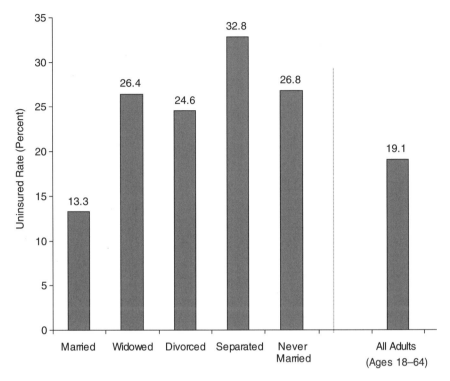

FIGURE 3.14 Probability of being uninsured for adults (ages 18–64 years), by marital status, 1999.
SOURCE: Rhoades and Chu, 2000.

based family coverage (Figures 3.15 and 3.16) (GAO, 1997a; GAO, 1997b). The uninsured rate for lower-income households is lower for families with children because some or all of the children may be eligible for and enrolled in Medicaid and SCHIP. Between 1976 and 1996, there was little change in children's uninsurance rates among two-parent working families, but there was an 8 percentage point increase in the uninsured rate for children in single-parent working families (Weinick and Monheit, 1999). Single parents tend to be young adults, which compounds the likelihood that they will lack coverage. Eligible children are more likely to participate in Medicaid if all family members have the opportunity to obtain coverage (Broaddus and Ku, 2000). However, 14 percent of all families with children are only partially insured (one or more members uninsured) and 10 percent are entirely without coverage (Hanson, 2001).

Lower-income parents face income and other eligibility criteria that may prevent them from qualifying for Medicaid, although their children may be covered. This may result in a family being partially insured. Since welfare reform in 1996, lower-income parents have been losing insurance coverage, with the de-

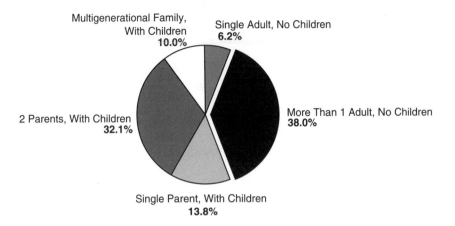

FIGURE 3.15 Distribution of uninsured population under age 65, by family composition, 1999. NOTE: Numbers may not add to 100.0 percent due to rounding.
SOURCE: Hoffman and Pohl, 2000

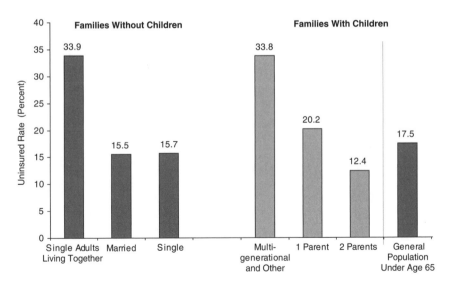

FIGURE 3.16 Probability of being uninsured for population under age 65, by family composition, 1999.
SOURCE: Hoffman and Pohl, 2000.

cline in public coverage greater than the increase in employment-based coverage. The impact falls disproportionately on lower-income mothers (Guyer and Mann, 1999; Garrett and Holahan, 2000; Klein, 2000; Guyer et al., 2001). Only 33 percent of women who move from public assistance to employment obtain coverage through their employer (Garrett and Holahan, 2000). Among low-income people (less than 100 percent of FPL), working parents are twice as likely to be uninsured as nonworking parents because nonworking, single parents often have very young children and are more likely to have Medicaid coverage (Guyer and Mann, 1999).

OTHER DEMOGRAPHIC DISPARITIES IN COVERAGE

The nature and type of labor force participation determine whether individuals and family members obtain employment-based coverage. Foreign-born persons and members of ethnic and racial minority groups are more likely than average to be uninsured, although their smaller numbers in the general population mean that uninsured rates overall are dominated by the rates for U.S.-born citizens and non-Hispanic whites.

Immigrant Status and Nativity

Most uninsured people are U.S. citizens by birth (native-born residents comprise about 90 percent of the general population). The relatively small proportion of the general population comprised of naturalized citizens and noncitizens (immigrants) is significantly more likely than U.S.-born residents to be uninsured, although immigrants' uninsured rates decline with increasing length of residency in the United States.

Residency status, family income, and length of residency in the United States are important influences on the likelihood that a person will lack insurance coverage (Carrasquillo et al., 2000). Foreign-born residents of the United States (including naturalized citizens, legal permanent residents, legal temporary residents, refugees, and undocumented immigrants) are almost three times as likely as U.S.-born residents to be uninsured, and among the foreign-born, noncitizens are more than twice as likely as citizens to be uninsured (Figures 3.17 and 3.18) (Mills, 2000).[5] Foreign-born residents are a relatively small proportion, about 10 percent, of the general population under age 65.[6] The declining uninsurance rate for

---

[5]Studies of immigrants' insurance status have only recent data to draw on, since the Census Bureau's Current Population Survey began collecting information about country of origin, date of arrival, and citizenship status in 1994 (Carrasquillo et al., 2000).

[6]The most recent Immigration and Naturalization Service estimate of the undocumented immigrant population is about 5 million people (as of October 1996). The annual growth in this number

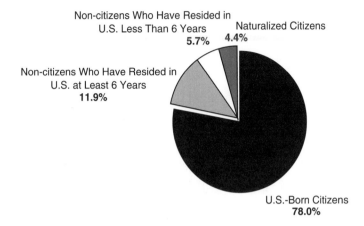

Estimated 42.1 Million Uninsured People = 100.0%

Non-citizens Who Have Resided in
U.S. Less Than 6 Years   Naturalized Citizens
5.7%   **4.4%**

Non-citizens Who Have Resided in
U.S. at Least 6 Years
11.9%

U.S.-Born Citizens
78.0%

FIGURE 3.17 Distribution of uninsured population under age 65, by immigrant status and nativity, 1999. NOTE: Numbers may not add to 100.0 percent due to rounding. SOURCE: Hoffman and Pohl, 2000.

immigrants with longer residence in the United States means that they contribute a relatively modest number and proportion to the overall growth in the uninsured population (Holahan et al., 2001).

Disparities in uninsured rates between immigrants and native-born U.S. residents reflect the lower rates of employment-based coverage among immigrants, which in turn is linked to greater-than-average likelihood employment in lower-waged positions (paying $7 or less per hour) and work in employment sectors with lower-than-average coverage rates (Carrasquillo et al., 2000).[7] Among full-time wage earners, 51 percent of noncitizen immigrants had employment-based coverage, compared with 76 percent of naturalized citizens and 81 percent of U.S.-born residents. Even among the lowest-waged full-time workers (earning less than $15,000 annually), 27 percent of noncitizen immigrants have employment-based

---

is projected to be approximately 275,000 persons per year (INS, 2001). This number represents about 1.9 percent of the general U.S. population for 1996.

There is little published national data about uninsured rates among undocumented immigrants. Studies that have evaluated local experiences with undocumented persons find that uninsured rates are much higher than for legal immigrants (Berk et al., 2000). For example, Project HOPE's 1996–1997 Hispanic Immigrant Health Care Access Survey of 972 undocumented immigrants in four cities (El Paso, Houston, Los Angeles, and Fresno) estimated an uninsured rate between 68 percent and 84 percent (Schur et al., 1999).

[7]This study followed immigrants from the 16 countries that contribute the largest numbers of immigrants to the United States.

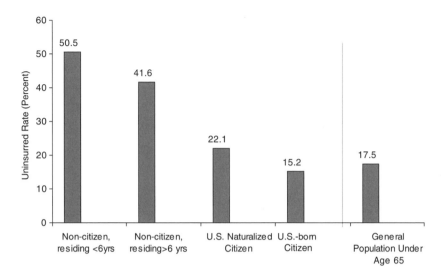

FIGURE 3.18 Probability of being uninsured for population under age 65, by immigrant status and nativity, 1999.
SOURCE: Hoffman and Pohl, 2000.

coverage, compared to 58 percent of U.S.-born residents (Carrasquillo et al., 2000). There is much variation in uninsured rates, reflecting the employment-based coverage of the sectors in which specific immigrant groups tend to concentrate. For example, there are concentrations of Mexican immigrant workers in agriculture, which has a higher-than-average uninsured rate, while Filipino immigrants often work in the health care industry, which has a lower-than-average uninsured rate.

For members of families headed by foreign-born persons who are not offered employment-based insurance and who are priced out of the individual insurance market, restrictive immigration and welfare policies enacted in the past five years have made public coverage increasingly difficult, if not impossible, to obtain. Since 1996, welfare and immigration reform legislation have banned legal immigrants who arrive after August 1996 from eligibility for Medicaid, SCHIP, and other federal means-tested benefits programs for their first five years in the United States, except for the financing of emergency care, with exceptions made for specific categories of persons including refugees (Rosenbaum, 2000).[8]

---

[8]With regard to Medicaid, the specific legislation includes the Personal Responsibility and Work Opportunity Reconciliation Act of 1996, as amended by the Illegal Immigration Reform and Immigrant Responsibility Act of 1996. The Balanced Budget Amendments Act of 1997 that established SCHIP excluded recently arrived (after August 1996) legal immigrant children from eligibility (Rosenbaum, 2000).

Both by design and in unintended ways (what many commentators describe as the "chilling effect" of the 1996 federal legislation), there was a steady decline in public coverage for lower-income, noncitizen immigrants between 1996 and 1999, contributing to an 8.5 percentage-point increase in their uninsured rate and a similar increase (8 percentage points) in the uninsured rate for U.S.-born children of legal immigrant parents (Ku and Matani, 2001). Children in immigrant families are more likely to be uninsured, whether or not their parents are citizens, although a child's status as a citizen reduces somewhat the probability of being uninsured (Brown et al., 1999). In lower-income working families, almost 20 percent of all U.S.-born children are uninsured, while slightly more than 50 percent of all foreign-born children are uninsured (Guendelman et al., 2001).

Race and Ethnicity

Non-Hispanic whites comprise about half of the uninsured, reflecting their majority in the general population. Non-Hispanic African Americans are twice as likely, and Hispanics three times as likely, as whites to be uninsured.

Higher uninsured rates among members of racial and ethnic minority groups are a consequence of lower rates of employment-based coverage and higher proportions of lower-income families within each group (Figures 3.19, 3.20, and 3.21). These rates are only partially offset by higher rates of public insurance coverage (Gabel, 1999; Brown et al., 2000a; Monheit and Vistnes, 2000; Shi, 2000b). Since the late 1970s, members of racial and ethnic minority groups have experienced a disproportionate decline in employment-based coverage (Gabel, 1999). For Hispanics, the declining rate also reflects changes related to declining family income levels and lower levels of educational attainment (Monheit and Vistnes, 2000). These changes are related to a shift in composition of the Hispanic population, with an increasing proportion comprised of immigrants from Central America and Mexico (Gabel, 1999; Monheit and Vistnes, 2000).

Hispanics

More than one-third of all Hispanics under age 65 are uninsured. Mirroring the uninsured population as a whole, more than one-half of uninsured Hispanics are members of families with at least one full-time, full-year worker, and more than eight out of ten are members of households with at least one part-time worker (Quinn, 2000). From 1987 through 1996, the number of uninsured Hispanics nearly doubled, reflecting both population growth and the decline of employment-based coverage (Monheit and Vistnes, 2000; Quinn, 2000).

The high uninsured rate for Hispanics reflects the fact that Hispanic wage earners are much less likely than average to be offered employment-based coverage and slightly more likely than non-Hispanic whites to decline to take up the offer (Cunningham, 1999a; Schur and Feldman, 2001). Since the mid-1970s,

Estimated 42.1 Million Uninsured People = 100.0

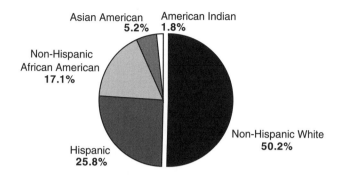

FIGURE 3.19 Distribution of uninsured population under age 65, by race and ethnicity, 1999. NOTE: Numbers may not add to 100.0 percent due to rounding.
SOURCE: Hoffman and Pohl, 2000.

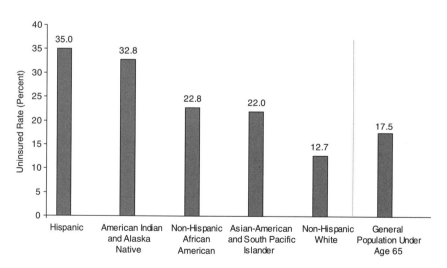

FIGURE 3.20 Probability of being uninsured for population under age 65, by race and ethnicity, 1999.
SOURCE: Hoffman and Pohl, 2000.

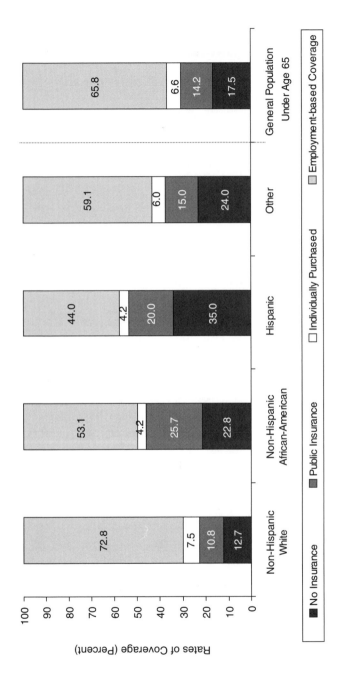

FIGURE 3.21 Sources of health insurance for population under age 65, by race and ethnicity, 1999. NOTE: Numbers may not add to 100.0 percent due to respondents reporting more than one source of coverage and due to rounding. SOURCE: Fronstin, 2000d.

Hispanic male wage earners uniquely have experienced a decline in offer rates for employment-based coverage (Monheit and Vistnes, 2000). Non-Hispanic whites in smaller firms are twice as likely to be offered coverage as are Hispanics (Quinn, 2000). The high uninsured rate for Hispanics also reflects a lower-than-average rate of public coverage for members of lower-income families. In families that earn less than the FPL, 45 percent of all Hispanics are uninsured, compared with 32 percent of non-Hispanic whites (Fronstin, 2000d).

In Hispanic families, 49 percent of members are covered by employment-based insurance plans: 59 percent are offered the chance to purchase coverage, and 83 percent take up this offer to enroll (Custer and Ketsche, 2000b). For members of families in which the primary wage earner is not offered employment-based coverage, 10 percent obtain employment-based coverage through other means, 2 percent purchase individual coverage, 23 percent obtain public insurance and 66 percent remain uninsured. For family members of primary wage earners who decline to purchase employment-based coverage, 34 percent receive employment-based coverage through other family members, 3 percent purchase individual coverage, 17 percent receive public insurance, and 46 percent remain uninsured (Custer and Ketsche, 2000b). The age distribution of Hispanics contributes to the high numbers of uninsured; the Hispanic population has a higher proportion of younger persons than older ones, and more than half of all Hispanic young adults go without health insurance (Hoffman and Pohl, 2000; Quinn, 2000).

Social and economic factors and nativity jointly contribute in important ways to the uninsured rate of the Hispanic population, because a significant proportion of this group are foreign-born or members of immigrant households. Among adult male wage-earning Hispanics, for example, Puerto Ricans and Cuban Americans have similar rates of private coverage, although Puerto Ricans have a higher employment-based coverage rate while Cuban Americans have a higher rate of individually purchased coverage (Fronstin et al., 1997). Mexican Americans have the lowest rate of private coverage compared to Puerto Ricans and Cuban Americans, reflecting lower wage levels and lower levels of education on average for Mexican Americans.

In addition, Hispanics who identify themselves as noncitizens are more than twice as likely to go without health insurance (58 percent uninsured rate) as Hispanic citizens (27 percent uninsured rate) (Brown et al., 2000a). If Hispanic children as a group had comparable citizenship and immigration status, parental educational attainment, work status, and family income as the rest of the population under age 18, they would still be more likely to be uninsured than non-Hispanic white, African-American, and Asian-American children (Weinick and Monheit, 1999).

American Indians and Alaska Natives

Almost one-third of all American Indians and Alaska Natives are

uninsured, a rate almost as high as that for Hispanics. There is little about the distinctive experiences of American Indians and Alaska Natives in the literature discussing insurance status and the uninsured population. There are few published population-level studies, and the survey data on which these studies are based may be weakened by small sample size since there are only 2.4 million self-identified American Indians and Alaska Natives (roughly 1 percent of the U.S. population); by inconsistencies in identifying and coding ethnic identity; and by a wide geographic range of residence (Brown et al., 2000a). It is important to note that in addition to or instead of insurance, some receive services directly through the Indian Health Service.

This high uninsured rate for Native Americans reflects a lower rate of employment-based coverage, higher-than-average unemployment rates, and lower-than-average wages for those who are employed. These three factors are only partially offset by a higher-than-average rate of public coverage by Medicaid and SCHIP. The federal Indian Health Service (IHS) delivers health care directly to persons who are recognized as American Indians or Alaska Natives. These services reach only about 20 percent of this population, mainly persons who live on reservations, who reside near the few urban IHS facilities around the country, and who belong to tribes that are federally recognized. The relatively low proportion of persons who obtain services from IHS reflects in part the predominantly urban location of this population (Brown et al., 2000a). Among Native Americans, 51 percent have employment-based coverage, compared with 73 percent of non-Hispanic whites, and individual insurance coverage is at one-fifth the rate of that for non-Hispanic whites (Brown et al., 2000a). About 17 percent of Native Americans have Medicaid, almost three times the rate of non-Hispanic whites (6 percent), reflecting the fact that Native Americans are about twice as likely to be members of lower-income families (Brown et al., 2000a). Yet almost half of all lower-income families in this group were uninsured, about twice the uninsured rate for lower-income families generally.

African Americans

Non-Hispanic African Americans are almost twice as likely as non-Hispanic whites to be uninsured (Fronstin, 2000d). From 1987 through 1996, the number of uninsured African Americans wage earners grew by 4.5 percentage points and the employment-based coverage rate declined, particularly for women wage earners (Monheit and Vistnes, 2000). Subsequent overall gains in employment-based coverage between 1994 and 1997 did not lower this uninsured rate substantially (Brown et al., 2000a).

Much of the high uninsured rate for African Americans is a consequence of a lower rate of employment-based coverage, even though primary wage earners in African-American families tend to work for larger-sized firms and in employment sectors with higher coverage (Brown et al., 2000a). In African American working families, 65 percent of their members have employment-based coverage: 77 percent are offered the chance to purchase coverage, and 86 percent take up this offer to enroll (Custer and Ketsche, 2000b). When employment-based coverage is not offered, 2 percent purchase individual coverage, 37 percent are covered by public insurance, and 49 percent remain uninsured. When a primary wage earner declines job-based coverage, 31 percent of family members obtain employment-based coverage through another family member, 3 percent purchase individual coverage, 29 percent obtain public insurance, and 37 percent remain uninsured (Custer and Ketsche, 2000b). When a family's primary wage earner has obtained employment-based coverage, the employment-based coverage rate for dependents is lower for African-American family members than for Hispanics (34 percent versus 43 percent, respectively) and the public coverage rate is higher (9 percent versus 5 percent) (Custer and Ketsche, 2000b). A lower proportion of African-American families have at least one full-time, full-year wage earner (58 percent, compared with 71 percent for non-Hispanic whites). Across all firm sizes, African Americans have lower employment-based coverage rates than non-Hispanic whites, with the disparity ranging from 14 to 30 percentage points (Brown et al., 2000a).

Across employment sectors, African Americans have lower employment-based coverage rates than non-Hispanic whites. For sectors with lower coverage such as agriculture and sales, 45 percent of African Americans are covered compared with 66 percent of non-Hispanic whites. For higher-coverage sectors such as manufacturing and professional services, 72 percent of African Americans are covered, compared with 86 percent of non-Hispanic whites (Brown et al., 2000a). Over time, African-American men have had a declining take-up rate for employment-based coverage, in comparison to non-Hispanic whites (Cunningham, 1999a; Custer and Ketsche, 2000b). This may reflect the increasing unaffordability of health insurance premiums for lower-income working families (Monheit and Vistnes, 2000).

The higher-than-average rate of public coverage for African Americans offsets some but not all of the disparity in employment-based health insurance coverage. This public coverage rate reflects the fact that 47 percent of all African Americans under age 65 are members of lower-income families, compared to about 20 percent of all non-Hispanic whites (Fronstin, 2000d). Public coverage rates are comparable for members of lower-income families, whether African American or non-Hispanic white, although African-American children have a higher participation rate in Medicaid (Brown et al., 2000a; Mills, 2000). African-American families with moderate or higher income levels, however, remain almost twice as likely as white non-Hispanics to be uninsured (Fronstin, 2000d).

Asian Americans and Pacific Islanders

There are disproportionately high uninsured rates among some eth-

nic groups collectively described as Asian American and Pacific Islander, reflecting the particular group's distinctive social, economic, and demographic characteristics and members' status as immigrants, refugees, or U.S.-born citizens (Brown et al, 2000a; Hoffman and Pohl, 2000). Rates for employment-based health insurance coverage vary considerably, with lower rates for Koreans and Vietnamese (and uninsured rates correspondingly high, greater than 30 percent) and higher rates for Japanese and families with residency extending over multiple generations (Carrasquillo et al., 2000). Generally, for Asian Americans and Pacific Islanders the rates of public insurance (Medicaid) are lower than those for other racial and ethnic groups, except for Southeast Asians, whose refugee status allows them to obtain public insurance coverage (Brown et al., 2000a).

Gender

More men than women are uninsured, and men are more likely than women to be uninsured.

Gender disparities in insurance coverage reflect the different experiences of men and women in the workplace and with public policies. There are more uninsured men (ages 18 through 64 years) than women, although women have a lower rate of employment-based coverage (Fronstin, 2000d). More women, on average, are eligible for public insurance because of their lower average income level and the greater likelihood that they may qualify for Medicaid during pregnancy or as the parent of infants and young children (Short, 1998). Most adults with Medicaid are women in lower-income families, for the most part pregnant women or the mothers of young children (Wyn et al., 2001). While fewer women than men go without coverage entirely, the greater number of women with individual insurance coverage and the higher number of women covered by public insurance are cause for concern, because such coverage tends to be unstable, thus creating more opportunities for gaps in coverage. (Miles and Parker, 1997; Fronstin, 2000d).

Both income and marital status are important influences on the likelihood that wage-earning women will be uninsured (Buchmueller, 1996–1997; Short, 1998). Single women are more likely to be offered employment-based health insurance than are single men (an offer rate of 78 compared to 72 percent), whereas married women are somewhat less likely than married men to be offered employment-based coverage. Lower take-up rates among married women wage earners, compared to married male wage earners (63 percent versus 72 percent) are a consequence of the greater likelihood that married women are insured as dependents on their spouse's health insurance policy (Buchmueller, 1996–1997, based on 1993 Current Population Survey data).

HOW GEOGRAPHIC DIFFERENCES AFFECT COVERAGE

The decentralized labor and health services markets in the United States, and the distinct public policies in each state and locality, together create unique contexts for the patterns already described for individuals and population groups. Differences among states with respect to population characteristics, industrial economic base, eligibility for public insurance, and relative purchasing power of family incomes shape the geographic disparities in insurance coverage rates (Marsteller et al., 1998; Rowland et al., 1998; Brown et al., 2000b; Cunningham and Ginsburg, 2001).

Region and State

The South and the West, the most populous regions, are home to the greatest numbers of uninsured persons (an estimated 17 million and 12 million, respectively). Residents of these regions are more likely than average to be uninsured.

The pattern is similar for persons at all income levels: Southerners and Westerners are more likely to be uninsured than are those who live in the North and Midwest (Figures 3.23, 3.24, and 3.25) (Fronstin, 2000d; Mills, 2000). Uninsured residents of California and Texas comprise more than one-quarter of the total number of uninsured persons, an estimated 12 million people (Hoffman and Pohl, 2000). New York and Florida are the third and fourth most populous states, respectively; their uninsured residents account for almost one-fifth of uninsured persons nationally. The remaining 47 jurisdictions (including the District of Columbia) are each estimated to contribute less than 4 percent of the total number of uninsured persons nationally.

There is much to be learned about what influences regional variation in uninsurance rates. A multivariate analysis of 60 communities across the United States, whose uninsured rates ranged from 5 to 29 percent, found that "population characteristics, employment, and unexplained or unmeasured geographic variations account for most of the differences" (Cunningham and Ginsburg, 2001). About one-third of the variation in uninsured rates is attributable to a combination of differences in racial and ethnic group composition (18 percent) and a combination of income and education (14 percent). About one-quarter of the difference is explained by employers' characteristics (21 percent) and employment rates (6 percent). Only about 13 percent of the difference among uninsured rates is explained by differences in Medicaid eligibility guidelines among the states.

Urban and Rural Areas

Reflecting the predominantly urban concentration of the U.S. population, most uninsured persons live in urban areas. Rural and urban residents, however, are about equally likely to be uninsured.

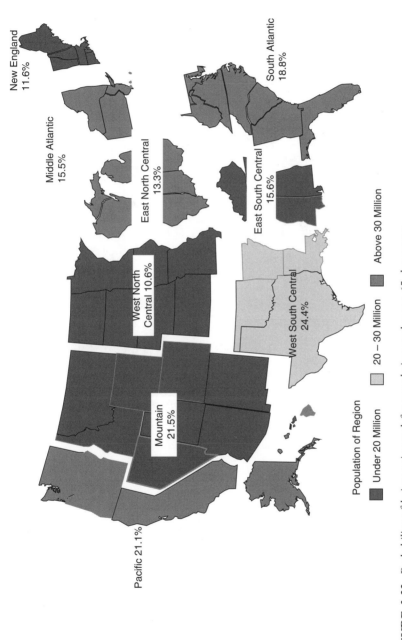

FIGURE 3.22 Probability of being uninsured for population under age 65, by census region, 1999. SOURCE: Fronstin, 2000d.

92

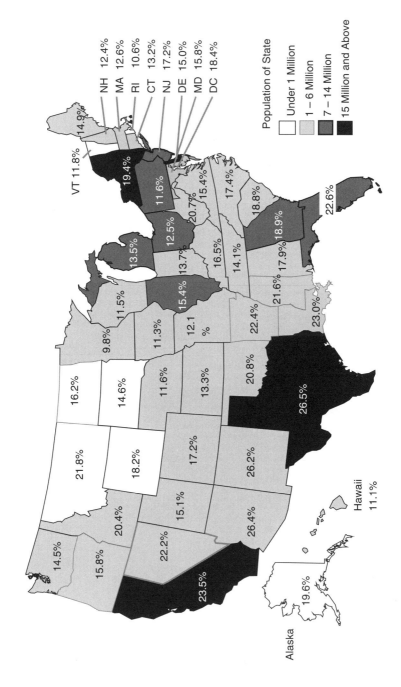

FIGURE 3.23 Probability of being uninsured for population under age 65, by state, 1997–1999.
SOURCE: Hoffman and Pohl, 2000.

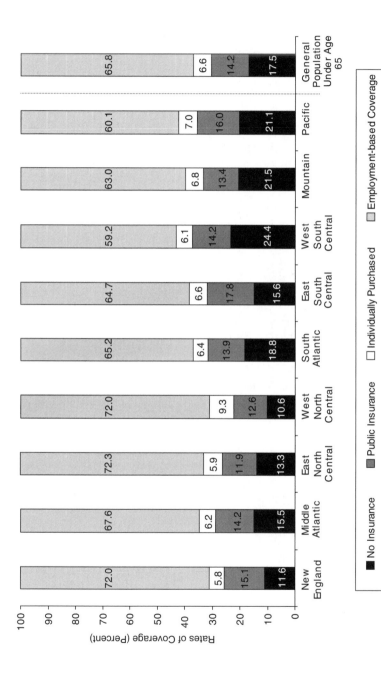

FIGURE 3.24 Sources of health insurance coverage for population under age 65, by census region, 1999. NOTE: Numbers may not add to 100.0 percent because individuals may report insurance from more than one source and due to rounding. SOURCE: Fronstin, 2000d.

More than four times as many uninsured persons live in urban as in rural areas, yet rural and urban residents have about the same chance of being uninsured (Figure 3.25).[9] As with other types of geographic comparisons, these general attributes mask underlying differences in local economies, health services infrastructure, public policies, and population characteristics that distinguish urban from rural areas (Hartley et al., 1994; Ormond et al., 2001). Although uninsured residents of rural areas are fewer in number, their presence is no less a concern. Similar to the overall trend in the 1990s, the number and proportion of uninsured among rural residents has increased (Pol, 2000).

Rural and urban areas differ in the mix of sources of coverage for their residents, with a higher private coverage rate in urban (71 percent) than in rural (68 percent) areas and a higher public coverage rate in rural areas (14 percent) compared to urban (11 percent) areas (Rhoades and Chu, 2000). The difficulties that small businesses face in purchasing affordable health insurance policies for their employees account for much of the disparity in coverage between rural and urban wage earners (Coburn et al., 1998; Mueller et al., 1998; Pol, 2000). In addition, rural uninsured workers are more likely to be employed by lower-waged firms, to work on a contingent basis, and to work in particular employment sectors (e.g., agriculture) with lower-than-average coverage rates. Even though there are greater numbers of lower-income uninsured persons among urban than among rural residents, rural uninsured workers are even more likely than their urban counterparts to earn relatively lower wages and to be members of lower-income families.

For urban areas, uninsured rates vary not only with differing population densities but also with the socioeconomic status of residents and with the presence of sizable immigrant communities (Brown et al., 2000b). The uninsured rates for the 85 largest metropolitan statistical areas (MSAs) range from 7 percent (Akron, Ohio, and Harrisburg, Pennsylvania) to 37 percent (El Paso, Texas) and employment-based coverage rates vary between 84 percent (Milwaukee, Wisconsin) and 49 percent (El Paso, Texas) (Brown et al., 2000b, based on 1997 data). Compared to the national average uninsured rate, 27 of these urban areas have significantly lower rates, while 12 have significantly higher rates.

---

[9]Definitions of urban and rural are not uniform. Differences in definitions and in survey methods may give differing estimates of the numbers of uninsured persons. The Current Population Survey (CPS) does not include a single variable to distinguish urban from rural areas.

• For the latter half of the 1990s, CPS data give higher uninsured rate estimates for urban compared with rural areas, while Medical Expenditure Panel Survey data give higher uninsured rate estimates for rural areas (Pol, 2000).

• There are two common and distinct ways to distinguish between urban and rural areas, one devised by the Office of Management and Budget and the other used by the CPS (Ricketts et al., 1999). In addition, there are coding schemes that differentiate among metropolitan statistical areas (MSAs), areas adjacent to MSAs, and areas that are not adjacent to MSAs (rural areas).

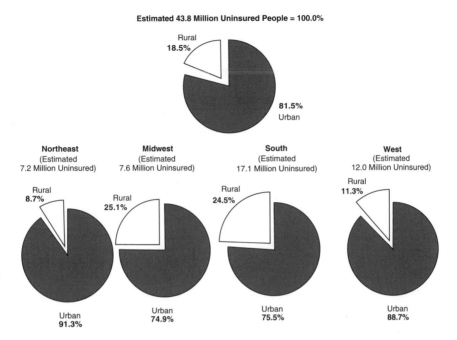

Estimated 43.8 Million Uninsured People = 100.0%

FIGURE 3.25 Distribution of uninsured population under age 65, by population density (rural or urban), 1998. NOTE: Numbers may not add to 100.0 percent due to rounding. SOURCE: Pol, 2000.

In MSAs with higher-than-average uninsured rates, a smaller proportion of people are wage earners and greater proportions of wage earners are employed in smaller firms. In addition, rates of unionization are lower, and greater proportions of wage earners are in employment sectors with relatively high uninsured rates, such as sales. The immigrant status of residents distinguishes MSAs with high uninsured rates from those with low uninsured rates. MSAs with high rates tend to have larger immigrant communities than those with low rates.[10]

Urban areas with high uninsured rates are home to greater proportions of people in lower-income families, and there is greater income inequality among residents (Brown et al., 2000b). Members of lower-income families are even more likely to be uninsured if they live in cities with high uninsured rates than they would be if they lived in cities with low uninsured rates (Brown et al., 2000b). Lower-income residents in urban areas with high uninsurance have a 30 percent employment-based coverage rate, compared with a 50 percent rate for those who

---

[10]These areas include Arizona (Phoenix-Mesa, Tucson), California (Los Angeles), Florida (West Palm Beach, Miami, Fort Lauderdale, Tampa), New Jersey (Jersey City), New York (New York), and Texas (El Paso, Dallas).

live in areas with low uninsured rates, and this disparity across urban areas remains even when racial and ethnic group identity and citizenship status are taken into account.

WHAT INFLUENCES AN UNINSURED RATE THE MOST?

If all things were equal, how much of the difference between uninsured rates could be attributed solely to social or economic characteristics or to differences in immigrant status or race and ethnicity? If all states were home to populations with similar characteristics, how much variation among the states in uninsured rates can be attributed to regional and local differences in industrial economies and health services markets or to state policies for public programs?

In this report, the discussions so far have been based on two-way comparisons, for example, between income level and the likelihood of being uninsured. These comparisons give us a general picture of the dynamics of insurance coverage but do not allow us to evaluate or rank the relative importance of one factor independently of all others. By using more sophisticated (multivariate) statistical methods, we can look at the influence of one or more characteristics at a time on the uninsured rate and better understand their distinct influences.[11] For example, both young adults and never married single persons have higher-than-average probabilities of being uninsured. Multivariate methods allow us to isolate the effect of youth from that of having never married.

In the multivariate analysis carried out by the Committee, much of the variation in uninsured rates among individuals and among population groups is associated with the following measured characteristics: income, occupation, employment sector and firm size of employer, education, health status, age, gender, race and ethnicity, citizenship status, and geography. However, large and statistically significant differences in uninsured rates remain after this analysis, and the variation in uninsured rates among population groups is not eliminated completely. For example, if Hispanics had the same probability of being uninsured as non-Hispanic whites with similar characteristics (except for ethnicity), the uninsured rate for Hispanics, which is about 22 percentage points higher than the uninsured rate for non-Hispanic whites, would be predicted to shrink to about a 7 percentage-point difference. The 15 percentage-point difference between the actual and predicted uninsured rates represents about a two-thirds decrease; thus, an estimated two-thirds of the difference in rates can be accounted for by differences in each group's measured socioeconomic, demographic (except for ethni-

---

[11]The small number of published multivariate statistical analyses in the research literature address more limited sets of questions than those explored by the Committee in its analysis presented here. See Appendix D for information about analysis and data.

city), health status, and geographic characteristics. The remaining difference between the two uninsured rates reflects unmeasured differences between these two population groups.

Differences in family income level account for a substantial portion of the difference in uninsured rates among groups in the general population. According to the Committee's multivariate analysis, the difference in uninsured rates between low-income families (less than 100 percent of FPL) and families with at least a moderate income (at least 200 percent of FPL) would decrease by one-third if these families resembled one another demographically, geographically, and in terms of health status.[12]

The level of educational attainment of a family's primary wage earner has an even larger independent effect. More than 40 percent of the difference in uninsured rates between families with primary wage earners who have not graduated from high school and families whose primary wage earners have post-college education would be eliminated if these families resembled one another demographically, geographically, and in terms of health status.[13]

Immigrant and nativity status have a pronounced influence on differences in uninsured rates among groups. Nearly 60 percent of the difference between uninsured rates for U.S.-born residents and naturalized citizens would disappear if naturalized citizens as a group shared the socioeconomic, demographic, health status, and geographic distribution characteristics of the U.S.-born population.[14] Differences between uninsured rates diminish when multivariate analysis is used to compare the population of long-term residents who are not citizens with persons born in the United States (a 26 percent decrease) and between short-term residents who are not citizens and U.S.-born residents (a 50 percent decrease).

Race and ethnicity play a significant role, both independently and together with immigrant and nativity status. If non-Hispanic African Americans as a group had the same measured characteristics as non-Hispanic whites, the difference between the uninsured rates for the two groups would decrease by roughly half.[15] When immigrant status is considered in addition to race and ethnicity, the size of these differences among the groups diminishes but remains significant. Differences in state uninsured rates shrink considerably if variations in the socioeconomic, demographic, and health status characteristics within each state's population are taken into account.[16] Given the limits of any statistical model, one would not expect differences among the states' uninsured rates to disappear completely. One

---

[12]See Appendix D for information about analysis and data.

[13]See Appendix D.

[14]See Appendix D.

[15]See Appendix D.

[16]The differences among uninsured rates for states reflect differences in individuals' characteristics rather than differences among states considered as a whole. See Appendix D for data and information about methods.

state with a higher-than-average uninsured rate, California, would have a reversal from a rate 4.9 percent above the national average to rate 1.0 percent below the national average. For states such as Hawaii with a lower-than-average uninsured rate, using multivariate analysis to compare populations results in an even lower-than-average rate (a 66 percent decrease).

SUMMARY

Who Goes Without Health Insurance?

A snapshot of the uninsured population gives us a portrait that reflects the relative size of population groups within the general population under age 65. More than 80 percent of uninsured persons are wage earners or members of working families, and two-thirds are members of lower-income families (earning less than 200 percent of FPL). Three-quarters of the uninsured are adults between the ages of 18 and 64, with one-half between the ages of 18 and 34 and one-quarter under the age of 18. Almost 80 percent are U.S.-born citizens, and half are non-Hispanic whites. Most are residents of the South and West, and three-quarters live in urban areas.

Who Is Most Likely to Go Without Coverage?

In bivariate analyses, a highly correlated set of socioeconomic factors exerts a key influence on the probability that a person will be uninsured. These factors include work status, family income, educational attainment, selected characteristics of a primary wage-earner's employer, and the age of a family's primary wage earner. Marital status and the presence of children each affect the potential opportunities for family members to obtain coverage. Coverage disparities for immigrants, for members of racial and ethnic minority groups, and to a lesser extent, for adult women, all reflect the importance of socioeconomic status, as well as the supporting roles played by public policies at the federal, state, and local levels. In addition, uninsured rates vary regionally and across the states. The presence of comparable uninsured rates between urban and rural areas can mask important differences in sources of coverage for rural and urban residents. In addition, a lower-income urban resident's chances of obtaining coverage decline if he or she lives in a city with a higher-than-average uninsured rate rather than in a city with a lower-than-average uninsured rate.

Socioeconomic, demographic, and geographic characteristics all have significant independent effects on the likelihood that one person will be uninsured compared to another. Differences in income, occupation, employment sector and firm size, education, health status, age, gender, race and ethnicity, citizenship status and length of residency, and geography account for much of the variability among people in their likelihood of being uninsured. Disparities in coverage rates persist among population groups, and not all of these differences can be accounted for by the commonly measured factors that most directly affect the chances of having health insurance.

The next and final chapter presents the Committee's analytic plan for tracing out the consequences of uninsurance. This plan will be fulfilled in the five reports that follow this one.

Box 4.1

In future reports the Committee will look at an array of consequences of uninsurance and address the distinctive effects on successively larger and more complex entities, from the individual to society as a whole. The conceptual framework developed in this first report will guide the analyses in each report, which will include examinations of health outcomes, financial impacts, and changes in quality of life that result from the lack of health insurance.

- *Report 2: Health Consequences for Individuals.* We know that insurance coverage improves access to health services, but what effects does the lack of health insurance have on health? The Committee will assess evidence about how being uninsured may affect many aspects of health for adults, including overall health status, disease-specific morbidity, avoidable hospitalizations, and mortality.

- *Report 3: Health and Economic Consequences for Families.* When a parent or child goes without health insurance, the consequences may be shared by the entire family. Because children depend on their parents or other adults to obtain health care for them, their parents' experiences with the health care system are important, as are the parents' beliefs about health care, their financial ability to purchase care, and their ability to negotiate that system on their children's behalf. The Committee will assess the published evidence about how a family's pattern of health insurance coverage affects both children's health and well-being and the family's economic stability and security.

- *Report 4: Consequences for Communities.* What are the health and economic consequences for communities of having large uninsured populations? In its fourth report the Committee will consider how the health and health services of communities are affected by the presence of substantial numbers of uninsured residents. The institutional and economic impacts of sizable uninsured populations will be examined for communities in both rural and urban areas and for communities with different types of economic bases.

- *Report 5: Economic Consequences for the Nation.* How much does it cost us as a nation to have roughly one out of every six or seven Americans uninsured? Who picks up the tab? Before policy makers can estimate what it may cost to change our current set of health financing arrangements, they will need a basis for comparison. The Committee will evaluate the costs of sustaining an uninsured population, both directly in terms of the health care provided them and indirectly in terms of increased burdens of disease and disability.

- *Report 6: Models and Strategies to Address the Consequences.* How can communities and public and private agencies solve the problems caused by lack of coverage? In its final report, the Committee will consider selected programs and proposals involving insurance-based strategies to expand coverage. Such strategies and models may be undertaken nationally, by states and localities, by government agencies, and by private businesses. The Committee will identify policy criteria to assess the features of alternative reform strategies.

4

Analytic Plan

This chapter describes the Committee's analytic plan to address the impacts and outcomes of our present structure of health insurance, the scope of the five future reports, and the schedule for their release. Each report in turn will focus successively on larger and more complex entities—the individual, the family, the local community, and the broader society. By proceeding systematically in this way, the Committee hopes to capture the distinctive effects of the lack of health insurance at each level of analysis. The conceptual framework discussed in Chapter 1 and presented in Appendix A will guide the analyses and be developed further in subsequent reports.

FUTURE COMMITTEE REPORTS

Report 2. Health Outcomes of People Who Lack Health Insurance

As already established by more than three decades of health services research, insurance coverage facilitates access to health care. The more that people have to pay out-of-pocket for a physician visit, prescription, or hospitalization, the less likely they are to seek such care. They are also likely to receive fewer services when they do seek care (Newhouse et al., 1993). In the extreme case of those with no insurance, people are less likely to receive health care when they need it compared to those with coverage. The second report will extend the understanding of the significance of health insurance coverage by examining personal health outcomes (including self-reported health status, disease-specific morbidity, avoidable hospitalizations, and mortality) in relation to whether or not a person has health insurance.

Studies that distinguish between those without coverage for shorter and longer periods of time and studies of the impact of losing health insurance coverage provide evidence of the effects of coverage on some health outcomes, in addition to the definitive findings regarding access to health care described in Chapter 1. For example, a study by Ayanian and colleagues (2000) identifies both difficulties in obtaining care and deficits in the quality of care for uninsured persons with specific chronic conditions. This study reports that adults who were uninsured for a year or longer were substantially less likely than those with coverage or those who were uninsured for shorter times to be screened for cancers, to receive services that reduce cardiovascular risks (e.g., hypertension, cholesterol screening and counseling about weight and smoking), and to receive regular care for diabetes, including foot and eye exams. These specific services are associated with improved longer-term health outcomes (Institute of Medicine, 2001).

Longitudinal studies following the same individuals over time can provide even more definitive evidence of the health effects of being uninsured, because unexamined characteristics of the study population are less likely to account for differences in outcomes between those with and those without insurance. In a study that followed a cohort of adult Medi-Cal beneficiaries who lost coverage in the mid-1980s, Lurie and colleagues found that both six months and one year after losing coverage, these persons reported poorer overall health and were less likely to have a usual source of care or believe that they could obtain care if needed than they had reported when participating in Medi-Cal. Former enrollees with hypertension had worse blood pressure control both at six months and one year than they had while enrolled in Medi-Cal (Lurie et al. 1984, 1986).

These are just two of literally hundreds of studies that have taken health insurance status into account as a characteristic that might affect a health outcome of some kind. Not all such studies have found a relationship between health insurance and health outcomes, and not all such studies are methodologically sound. The second report will present and use explicit criteria to assess evidence of the impact of health insurance status on individual adult health outcomes. The conceptual model discussed earlier will guide the analysis. *The second report, on health outcomes, will be issued in the spring of 2002.*

Report 3. Family Impacts of Lacking Health Insurance

In almost a quarter of all American families with children, at least one family member lacks health insurance (Hanson, 2001). An estimated 10 million children under the age of 18 remain uninsured, despite enactment of the State Children's Health Insurance Program (SCHIP) in 1997. Because children depend on their parents or other adults to obtain health care for them, parents' experiences with the health care system, their beliefs about health care, and their ability to negotiate that system on their children's behalf are important. Providing health insurance to children removes one barrier to access to care, but it may do little to remove other barriers that spring from the family context. Furthermore, if the health of uninsured adults suffers as a result of impeded access to care, their ability to care for their children may also be adversely affected. Finally, when one or more family member lacks coverage for health care, the entire family is exposed to potentially catastrophic financial costs. Even when confronted with less catastrophic illness, uninsured families are significantly more likely to have high out-of-pocket medical expenses than are privately insured or Medicaid-enrolled families, although privately insured families are likely to pay more in health insurance premiums (Davidoff et al., 2000).

The Committee will review and document the effects on families when one or more members lack health insurance. It will address the circumstances of and impacts on special populations and various family structures. The report will examine a variety of effects, including measures of family members' health and of children's developmental status, access to and use of health services, financial burdens, and family psychosocial stress. Taking the family as the primary unit of analysis, the report will identify patterns of health insurance coverage within families in order to discern relationships between parents' insurance and health status and their children's health insurance status, use of health services, and health. The report will also examine health insurance status in relation to the family's out-of-pocket costs for medical care and its financial well-being and stability. The research literature on health outcomes for children who have gained health insurance coverage in recent expansions of Medicaid and with SCHIP will be synthesized in the report. *The third report, on family impacts, will be issued in the fall of 2002.*

Report 4. Community-wide Effects of Uninsured Populations

The presence of substantial numbers of uninsured people may adversely affect communities as well as the uninsured individuals and their families. The "spillover" effects on the insured population and the community at large could be considerable, although these are not well documented or understood. Faced with a need for health care, some people without health insurance seek the care they need and pay for it out-of-pocket, some try to obtain the care at subsidized rates or at public expense, and some forgo care. The result for the individual is often poorer than that obtained by people with insurance coverage. Several sources estimate that uninsured persons obtain about two-thirds of the care of comparable insured populations (Marquis and Long, 1994–1995). The fourth report will focus on the often indirect and hidden costs to communities of serving those without insurance.

Physicians working in private practice, nonprofit clinics such as federally qualified health centers (FQHCs), government-sponsored primary care and specialty clinics, and hospitals all provide significant amounts of subsidized or free care. Institutional providers such as hospitals and clinics must obtain funds to cover the costs of subsidized care from revenue generated from paying patients (cost shifting), tax-based subsidies, or private philanthropy. Thus, one set of community impacts may include higher prices, higher taxes, or dependence on philanthropy to support care for persons without health insurance.

Other community consequences result from the financial burden placed on providers who treat large numbers of uninsured patients. These effects may include cutbacks in service, closure or relocation of services, overcrowded emergency rooms, and relocation of physicians' offices or even hospitals from areas of town that have concentrations of uninsured persons. These disruptions may reduce people's access to care regardless of their insurance status. A third potential impact of uninsured populations on communities follows from the failure to obtain needed health care for communicable diseases, such as treatment for tuberculosis or diagnosis of HIV infection. Although these effects have not been well documented by published research, the Committee intends to investigate available sources of information to examine whether there are public costs related to preventable disability and an increased incidence of communicable diseases related to uninsured populations.

The report will identify the nature and magnitude of effects on geographically defined communities in which differing proportions of the population lack health insurance with a focus on communities (municipalities, metropolitan areas, rural areas, states) that have disproportionately large uninsured populations. Impacts in rural communities may differ from those in urban areas and will be examined in some detail. The Committee will document the relationships of community uninsured rates to economic and industrial characteristics, public health and welfare programs, population demographics, and health care professional and institutional resources. Specifically, the report may explore the relationship between community levels of uninsurance and the general availability and quality of physician services, emergency medical services, and highly specialized institutional services such as trauma, burn, and intensive care units. *The fourth report, on community impacts, will be issued in the winter of 2003.*

Report 5. Economic Costs of an Uninsured Population

The fifth report will estimate various economic costs incurred by society resulting from the fact that a significant percentage of the U.S. population lacks health insurance. Whereas the previous report on community impacts will examine local costs, both economic and other kinds, the fifth report will consider a broader array of financial impacts on individuals, families, and the national economy. To the extent possible, the analysis will include estimates of selected direct costs of providing health care to the uninsured, increased costs resulting from the inefficient use of health services, and the indirect costs of preventable disability and lost productivity among uninsured persons with specific health conditions. The report will explore how the burden of costs is paid, including out-of-pocket payments by the uninsured and their families, uncompensated care by health care providers and institutions, tax levies by all levels of government, higher health insurance premiums to support cost shifting, gifts from philanthropies, and the indirect cost of disability on business operations. The report will present a clearer understanding of the extent to which society already pays to care for the uninsured. *The fifth report, on economic costs, will be issued in the spring of 2003.*

Report 6. Strategies and Models for Providing Health Insurance

In its final report, the Committee will examine selected state, local, federal, and private-sector policies and programs that have attempted to mitigate the adverse impacts of lack of health insurance on individuals, families, health care providers, and communities by expanding insurance coverage. The report will identify promising prototypes as well as innovative approaches to the problem of uninsurance. A goal of the report will be to identify policy criteria that can be used to assess the merits of alternative reform strategies, rather than to endorse or recommend specific reform approaches. *The sixth report, on model programs and policies, will be issued in late summer of 2003.*

Appendixes

A

A Conceptual Framework for Evaluating the Consequences of Uninsurance: A Cascade of Effects

The Committee's conceptual framework for evaluating the consequences of uninsurance is depicted in Figure A.1. This three-part framework is based on an economic model of insurance status and the impact of out-of-pocket costs on health care demand. Both have been linked to Andersen's model of access to health services, which incorporates ideas from the behavioral sciences to understand the processes of health services delivery and health-related outcomes for individuals (Andersen and Davidson, 2001).

The framework uses the Andersen model's grouping of variables into three categories: (1) resources that foster or enable the process of obtaining health care; (2) personal or community characteristics that favor or predispose action related to obtaining health care; and (3) needs for health care, as articulated by those in need, determined by health care providers, or identified by researchers and decision makers. Arrows and spatial relationships among the boxes indicate hypothesized causal and temporal relationships. For example, a woman might have insurance coverage for a mammography screening, but if she has no regular source of care and lives 20 miles from the nearest facility offering such service, she could face obstacles to obtaining care. This case can be followed through the model, as shown below.

For the purposes of this study, the Committee linked Andersen's model to determinants of health insurance status. These changes to the model allow one to characterize not only individual- and population-level health indicators, but also economic measures of family well-being, institutional viability, and community-level socioeconomic conditions. In addition, depicting the economic consequences of uninsurance allows the Committee to assess hypothesized interactions between

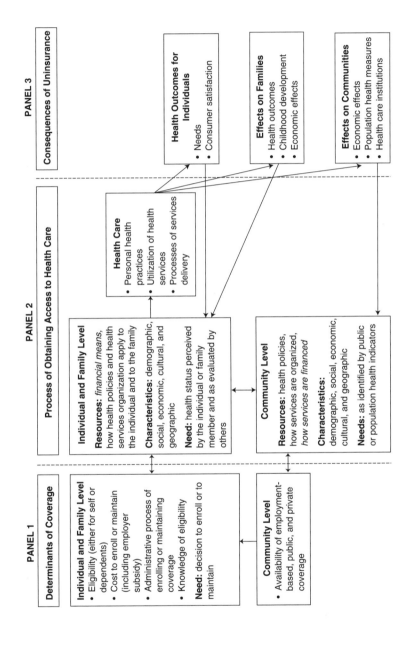

PANEL 1

Determinants of Coverage

Individual and Family Level
- Eligibility (either for self or dependents)
- Cost to enroll or maintain (including employer subsidy)
- Administrative process of enrolling or maintaining coverage
- Knowledge of eligibility

Need: decision to enroll or to maintain

Community Level
- Availability of employment-based, public, and private coverage

PANEL 2

Process of Obtaining Access to Health Care

Individual and Family Level

Resources: *financial means*, how health policies and health services organization apply to the individual and to the family

Characteristics: demographic, social, economic, cultural, and geographic

Need: health status perceived by the individual or family member and as evaluated by others

Community Level

Resources: health policies, how services are organized, *how services are financed*

Characteristics: demographic, social, economic, cultural, and geographic

Needs: as identified by public or population health indicators

Health Care
- Personal health practices
- Utilization of health services
- Processes of services delivery

PANEL 3

Consequences of Uninsurance

Health Outcomes for Individuals
- Needs
- Consumer satisfaction

Effects on Families
- Health outcomes
- Childhood development
- Economic effects

Effects on Communities
- Economic effects
- Population health measures
- Health care institutions

FIGURE A.1 A conceptual framework for evaluating the consequences of uninsurance—a cascade of effects. NOTE: Italics indicate terms that include direct measures of health insurance coverage.

economics and health and, in particular, the growing literature on the psychosocial dimensions of family well-being and childhood development.

PANEL 1: DETERMINANTS OF COVERAGE

The left third of Figure A.1 addresses the key determinants that influence the coverage status of individuals and families. Individual- and family-level characteristics include financial resources, categorical eligibility for public health insurance, labor market characteristics associated with employment-based insurance, and the requisite skills to enroll and maintain coverage. In the example, the woman's eligibility for coverage of mammography screening would be an individual determinant of coverage, the top box in Panel 1. In the model, community-level factors include public program eligibility standards, labor market characteristics that determine the availability of employment-based health insurance, and the commercial market for individual health insurance. This is a condensed version of the detailed figure on determinants of eligibility and enrollment (Figure 2.2), and the logic laid out in Chapter 2.

PANEL 2: PROCESS OF OBTAINING ACCESS TO HEALTH SERVICES

The center third of Figure A.1 is based on Andersen's model of access to health care (Andersen and Davidson, 2001). The boxes labeled "community level" and "individual and family level" each contain aggregate and individual-level variables, respectively, believed to influence how people obtain access to health care. Community-level variables describe the context or environment within which individuals and their families seek and use health care. Because health care services are provided and consumed locally, the term "community" refers to a residential or geographic grouping. The woman discussed earlier lived 20 miles from a mammography site, a factor that would be included in the lower left box of Panel 2.

Implicit in grouping variables into the categories of resources, characteristics, and needs are judgments about how much a particular variable may be susceptible to change. Variables labeled as "resources" are considered, at least theoretically, to be more open to change. Those termed "characteristics" are considered less flexible or manipulable, and those called "needs" comprise a mixed or heterogeneous grouping, with some needs being more changeable than others.

As a whole, community-level and individual- and family-level variables describe many potential scenarios for accessing health care. The variables within the box labeled "health care" describe how these potentials may be realized, with particular attention to the role of health insurance coverage. The process of health care delivery is characterized in terms of three types of variables: (1) personal health practices (e.g., dietary habits, physical exercise), (2) the use of health services (e.g., number and kind of physician visits within a year), and (3) processes of care (e.g., adherence to clinical practice guidelines). In the example given, the woman's lack of a regular source of care would fall into this box on the right of Panel 2. The Committee focuses most of its attention on the literature concerning the processes of services delivery and the utilization of health services while recognizing that personal health practices may be influenced by insurance coverage and access to care.

PANEL 3: HOW HEALTH INSURANCE INFLUENCES HEALTH OUTCOMES AND AFFECTS FAMILIES AND COMMUNITIES

The right side of Figure A.1 describes the ways in which the Committee anticipates that health insurance status may affect the health, economic, and social characteristics of individuals, families, and communities, by means of access to and utilization of health care. These effects of *realized access* to health care cascade from the smallest unit of analysis, the individual, to increasingly larger units, first that of the family and then the community. The consequences linked to health insurance influence community-level and individual- and family-level variables that describe the process of obtaining access to health care and also of gaining or losing health insurance coverage. The process is dynamic with multiple feedbacks. Employment status and income influence insurance status, which affects current and future health status. This in turn can influence employment status, bringing us full circle. The woman discussed in the example might have a malignant lump that goes undetected because the obstacles mentioned above deter her from seeking a screening mammogram. She could undergo more extensive surgery and related treatments than would have been necessary if the lump had been detected earlier. This would be a negative health outcome (the top box in Panel 3) that might affect her family in serious ways (middle box of Panel 3) and might also affect her eligibility for health insurance in the future (back to Panel 1, top box).

This conceptual framework provides a basis for discussing many variables related to health insurance coverage in this report. It will also serve to guide analyses for the Committee's future reports. As the Committee focuses on specific issues, such as health outcomes or the effects on families, specific pieces of the model will be discussed in more detail.

B

Measuring Insurance Coverage and Insurance Rates

A number of publicly and privately sponsored surveys provide information about insurance coverage and estimates of the number of uninsured Americans. The structure and features of these surveys are summarized in Table B.1. This discussion addresses issues that are generally associated with measuring insurance coverage in surveys by describing them in relation to the Current Population Survey (CPS).

The most commonly used survey is the CPS, conducted by the U.S. Census Bureau. The CPS provides relatively timely reports, traditionally reporting every September about insurance coverage during the previous calendar year. The Committee's report relies primarily on estimates produced by the CPS because of its annual updates and its usefulness in analyzing trends over time. The other surveys described in Table B.1 have been used to address questions that may be difficult or impossible to answer using CPS data alone.

The CPS is the principal source of information on labor force characteristics of the civilian, noninstitutionalized population in the United States. It is perhaps most widely known as the source of data for the monthly unemployment rate. Each month, about 50,000 households, representing approximately 130,000 individuals, are interviewed. In 2001, an additional 30,000 households are to be interviewed to provide more precise state-level estimates of the number uninsured. Despite the short (six- to seven-month) turnaround from data collection to publication, the uninsured rates published each September do not reflect the most recent economic trends, because the CPS reporting period for individuals' insurance status begins 21 months before coverage rates are published.

A supplement every March collects income information for households, families, and individuals. In 1980, the March supplement to the CPS began to ask questions about health insurance. Until the March 2000 survey, the CPS did not ask individuals directly if they were uninsured. Instead, it asked about a series of coverage types such as private insurance and Medicare. Those individuals who did not acknowledge any form of coverage were counted as uninsured.

In the March 2000 CPS an experimental question was added to the interview to verify whether a person was uninsured throughout the previous year. While the results from the experimental questions were not known when this report went to press, it is likely that the Census will revise its uninsured estimate downward, making the CPS estimates more consistent with other surveys such as the Community Tracking Survey and the National Survey of American Families that do use a verification question.

Issues that arise in the CPS include the following:

• *Recall period.* The CPS asks if someone was covered by a particular form of health insurance at any time over the previous year. It appears that respondents answer the question in different ways. Some may report coverage status at the time of the interview, rather than over the previous calendar year. Some may not accurately recall when coverage began or ended and thus fail to report coverage during the period in question (Lewis et al., 1998.)

• *Household and family definition.* The CPS defines households as all persons under a roof and family members as all related persons in a household. A family unit for health insurance purposes tends to consist of fewer persons than all who live in a household. For example, a single parent and children may live with the child's grandparents, but the grandchildren would be unlikely to be eligible for health insurance coverage through their grandparents' employers.

• *Underreporting participation in public programs.* Although the CPS uses state program names when asking about Medicaid, and thus refers to Medi-Cal in California and MediPass in Florida, CPS data show fewer people participating in Medicaid than do administrative records for the program.

TABLE B.1 Summary of National Surveys Compiling Information on Health Insurance Status of the Population (Estimates for Population Under Age 65)

Survey and Sponsor	Frequency of Survey	Sample	Methods	Who Counts As "Uninsured"	Estimated Uninsured and Period Uninsured[a]
Current Population Survey— U.S. Census Bureau	Annual; health insurance-related questions since 1980	50,000 households; 116,000 individuals. Additional 30,000 households beginning in 2001	National probability sample with independent state-level samples allowing for state-level estimates. Telephone and face-to-face interviews. One person answers on behalf of household members	Residual— persons not reporting any type of coverage[b]	1999 42.1 million; uninsured throughout prior calendar year
Survey of Income and Program Participation— U.S. Census Bureau	New panel every 2–4 years since 1983. Monthly data based on quarterly interviews	36,700 households with 94,997 persons in 1996 panel	In-person interviews with each household member over age 15; adults asked about children	Residual— persons not reporting any type of coverage	10/94-10/95 35 million; monthly; months combined for annual estimates of monthy uninsured

continued

TABLE B.1 *Continued*

Survey and Sponsor	Frequency of Survey	Sample	Methods	Who Counts As "Uninsured"	Estimated Uninsured and Period Uninsured[a]
Medical Expenditure Panel Survey—Agency for Healthcare Research and Quality	New in 1996; two panels (1996–1997 and 1997–1998) to date. Comparable prior surveys: National Medical Expenditure Survey, 1987; National Medical Care Expenditure Survey, 1977	13,087 families and 32,636 persons in 1997	National probability sample. Six interviews over 30 months. Computer-assisted in-person and telephone interviews	Residual—persons not reporting any type of coverage	1996 32 million uninsured throughout calendar year, 44 million uninsured throughout 3–6 month period; reports provide status during a reference period of 4–6 months; data allows for monthly analysis
Behavioral Risk Factor Surveillance System—State health departments and the Centers for Disease Control and Prevention (CDC)	Ongoing set of surveys carried out in each state; health insurance questions began in 1991	Approximately 150,000 adults per year	State-level sampling of telephone numbers. One adult per household, thus no data on children	Answer "no" to question about having health coverage	1998 22 million adults ages 18–64 years (survey excludes children); uninsured at time of interview

National Health Interview Survey—National Center for Health Statistics, CDC	Annual; health insurance questions made part of each year's survey in 1997	43,000 households containing 106,000 individuals	National probability sample with in-person interviews with each family as a group	Individuals reporting no insurance type asked to verify that they are uninsured	1997 36 million; uninsured at time of interview
National Survey of America's Families—Urban Institute	First conducted in 1997 and again in 1999	44,000 households with 106,000 individuals	Telephone survey of nationally representative sample of persons under 65, also representative for 13 states, with in-person interviews of a sample of households without telephones	Individuals reporting no insurance type asked to verify that they are uninsured	1997 36 million; uninsured at time of interview
Community Tracking Study—Center for Studying Health System Change	Two-year cycle, beginning 1996–1997	33,000 households; 60,446 individuals in first survey	Telephone survey of nationally representative sample in 60 randomly selected metropolitan statistical areas (MSAs); more intensive sampling in 12 of these MSAs	Individuals reporting no insurance type asked to verify that they are uninsured	7/96–7/97 35 million; uninsured at time of interview

aEstimates from surveys as reported in Fronstin, 2000a.

bBeginning in March 2000, an additional question was added to the survey, to confirm that the respondent intended to report being uninsured for the previous year. Estimates that take this verification question into account are expected to be released by the U.S. Census Bureau in August 2001. It is anticipated that the estimates of the number of uninsured persons in 2000, to be released in September 2001, will be based on the results of the new verification question.

C

Data Tables

TABLE C.1 Distribution of the Uninsured Population Under Age 65 and Probabilities of Going Without Coverage, by Family Income Level and by Federal Poverty Level, 1999

	No. in Population (<65 yrs) (millions)	% Distribution in Population	No. Uninsured (est.) (millions)	% Distribution Uninsured	% Uninsured Rate
Totals	240.7	100.0	42.1	100.0	17.5
People (ages 0–64) by yearly family income level					
<$10,000	21.4	8.9	8.1	19.2	37.8
$10,000–$19,999	27.1	11.3	9.0	21.3	33.2
$20,000–$29,999	27.6	11.5	6.8	16.1	24.6
$30,000–$39,000	27.2	11.3	5.3	12.5	19.4
$40,000–$49,000	24.1	10.0	3.3	7.9	13.9
At least $50,000	113.3	47.1	9.7	22.9	8.5
People (ages 0–64) by federal poverty level (FPL)					
<100% FPL	39.7	16.5	15.4	36.5	38.7
100%–199% FPL	42.0	17.5	12.1	28.7	28.8
(<200%FPL)	81.7	33.9	27.5	65.3	33.6
200%–299% FPL	39.1	16.2	6.3	15.1	16.2
At least 300% FPL	119.8	49.8	8.3	19.8	6.9
FPL by family size for 1999 in the lower 48 states	100% FPL =	200% FPL =	300% FPL =		
1-person family	8,240	16,480	24,720		
2-person family	11,060	22,120	33,180		
3-person family	13,880	27,760	41,640		
4-person family	16,700	33,400	50,100		

SOURCES: Fronstin, 2000d, Table 6; Hoffman and Pohl, 2000, Table 7; U.S. Department of Health and Human Services, 1999.

TABLE C.2 Distribution of Uninsured Adult Population Ages 19–64 Years and Probabilities of Going Without Coverage, by Level of Educational Attainment, 1999

	No. in Population (<65 yrs) (millions)	% Distribution in Population	No. Uninsured (est.) (millions)	% Distribution Uninsured	% Uninsured Rate
Totals	164.4	100.0	31.3	100.0	19.0
Less than high school	21.5	13.1	8.4	26.8	39.0
High school graduate	53.4	32.5	11.3	36.1	21.2
Some college	47.8	29.1	7.8	24.9	16.4
At least a college graduate	41.5	25.2	3.8	12.1	9.1

SOURCE: Hoffman and Pohl, 2000, Table 30.

TABLE C.3 Distribution of Uninsured Population Under Age 65 and Probabilities of Going Without Coverage, by Work Status of Self or of Primary Wage Earner, for All Families and for Lower-Income Families, 1999

	No. in Population (<65 yrs) (millions)	% Distribution in Population	No. Uninsured (est.) (millions)	% Distribution Uninsured	% Uninsured Rate
By work status of wage earner					
Totals	240.7	100.0	42.1	100.0	17.5
2 full-time	72.5	30.1	6.6	15.7	9.1
1 full-time	130.1	54.0	23.2	55.1	17.9
1 part-time	15.3	6.4	4.9	11.6	31.9
No wage earners	22.8	9.5	7.4	17.6	32.5
By work status of wage earner, for lower-income families					
Totals	81.7	100.0	27.5	100.0	33.6
2 full-time	7.6	9.4	2.2	8.2	29.3
1 full-time	42.8	52.4	14.1	51.2	32.8
1 part-time	11.4	14.0	4.2	15.2	36.6
No wage earners	19.8	24.3	7.0	25.4	35.2

SOURCE: Hoffman and Pohl, 2000, Tables 7 and 8.

TABLE C.4 Distribution of Uninsured Wage Earners Under Age 65 and Probabilities of Going Without Coverage, by Selected Characteristics of Employer, 1999

	No. in Population (<65 yrs) (millions)	% Distribution in Population	No. Uninsured (est.) (millions)	% Distribution Uninsured	% Uninsured Rate
Totals	138.5	100.0	24.2	100.0	17.5
By size of employer's firm					
Self-employed	12.5	9.0	3.1	12.6	24.5
Public sector	20.0	14.4	1.5	6.1	7.4
Private sector employees	106.0	76.5	19.6	81.2	18.5
Private sector, <10 workers	15.3	11.0	5.0	20.7	32.8
Private sector, 10–24 workers	11.4	8.2	3.0	12.3	26.2
Private sector, 25–99 workers	16.4	11.8	3.4	14.1	20.7
Private sector, 100–499 workers	16.7	12.0	2.6	10.6	15.4
Private sector, 500–999 workers	6.2	4.5	0.8	3.3	12.9
Private sector, at least 1,000 workers	40.1	30.0	4.9	20.2	12.2
By employer's employment sector					
Agriculture, forestry, fishing, mining, construction	12.8	9.2	4.1	17.1	32.2
Manufacturing	29.4	21.2	3.9	16.1	13.3
Trade (wholesale, retail)	46.3	33.4	10.0	41.4	21.6
Personal services	29.9	21.6	4.7	19.3	15.6
Public sector	20.0	14.4	1.5	6.1	7.4

SOURCE: Fronstin, 2000d, Tables 3 and 4.

TABLE C.5 Distribution of Uninsured Population Under Age 65 and Probabilities of Going Without Coverage, by Age, 1999

	No. in Population (<65 yrs) (millions)	% Distribution in Population	No. Uninsured (est.) (millions)	% Distribution Uninsured	% Uninsured Rate
Totals	240.7	100.0	42.1	100.0	17.5
By age					
0–17	72.3	30.0	10.0	23.8	13.9
18–64	168.4	70.0	32.1	76.2	19.1
By age					
<6	23.6	9.8	3.3	7.8	13.9
6–12	28.7	11.9	3.8	9.0	13.4
13–17	20.0	8.3	2.9	6.9	14.5
18–24	26.4	11.0	7.7	18.3	29.2
25–34	37.5	15.6	8.8	20.9	23.3
35–44	44.5	18.5	7.4	17.6	16.6
45–54	36.6	15.2	4.9	11.6	13.4
55–64	23.4	9.7	3.4	8.1	14.5

SOURCE: Fronstin, 2000d, Table 10.

TABLE C.6 Distribution of Uninsured Population Under Age 65 and Probabilities of Going Without Coverage, by Family Composition, 1999

	No. in Population (<65 yrs) (millions)	% Distribution in Population	No. Uninsured (est.) (millions)	% Distribution Uninsured	% Uninsured Rate
Totals	240.7	100.0	42.1	100.0	17.5
By presence of children					
Families without children	90.0	37.3	18.6	44.2	20.7
Families with children	150.6	62.6	23.5	55.9	15.6
By family composition					
Single adult, no children	16.5	6.8	2.6	6.2	15.7
More than 1 adult in family, no children	73.5	30.5	16.0	38.0	21.8
Single-parent family	28.9	12.0	5.8	13.8	20.2
Two-parent family	109.3	45.4	13.5	32.1	12.4
Multigenerational family	12.4	5.2	4.2	10.0	33.8

SOURCE: Hoffman and Pohl, 2000, Table 7.

TABLE C.7 Distribution of Uninsured Adults (Ages 16–64 Years) and Probabilities of Going Without Coverage, by Marital Status, 1999

	No. in Population (<65 yrs) (millions)	% Distribution in Population	No. Uninsured (est.) (millions)	% Distribution Uninsured	% Uninsured Rate
Totals	174.6	100.0	34.0	100.0	19.5
Married	92.6	38.8	12.3	29.0	13.3
Widowed	3.2	1.3	0.8	n/a	26.4
Divorced	19.5	8.2	4.8	11.3	24.6
Separated	4.0	1.7	1.3	n/a	32.8
Never married	55.3	23.2	14.8	34.9	26.8

SOURCE: Rhoades and Chu, 2000, Tables 2 and 4.

TABLE C.8 Distribution of the Uninsured Population Under Age 65 and Probabilities of Going Without Coverage, by Race and Ethnicity, 1999

	No. in Population (<65 yrs) (millions)	% Distribution in Population	No. Uninsured (est.) (millions)	% Distribution Uninsured	% Uninsured Rate
Totals	240.7	100.0	42.1	100.0	17.5
Non-Hispanic white	165.9	68.9	21.1	50.2	12.7
Non-Hispanic African American	31.6	13.1	7.2	17.1	22.8
Hispanic	31.0	12.9	10.9	25.8	35.0
Asian/S. Pacific Islander	9.9	4.1	2.2	5.2	22.0
American Indian/Alaskan Native	2.3	1.0	0.8	1.8	32.8

SOURCE: Hoffman and Pohl, 2000, Table 7.

TABLE C.9 Distribution of Uninsured Population Under Age 65 and Probabilities of Going Without Coverage, by Immigrant and Nativity Status, for All Incomes and For Lower-Income Families, 1999

	No. in Population (<65 yrs) (millions)	% Distribution in Population	No. Uninsured (est.) (millions)	% Distribution Uninsured	% Uninsured Rate
For all incomes					
Totals	240.7	100.0	42.1	100.0	17.5
U.S. born (citizen)	215.5	89.5	32.9	78.0	15.2
Naturalized citizen	8.4	3.5	1.9	4.4	22.1
Non-citizen, residing <6 years	4.7	2.0	2.4	5.7	50.5
Non-citizen, residing at least 6 years	12.1	5.0	5.0	11.9	41.6
For members of lower-income families					
Totals	81.7	100.0	27.5	100.0	33.6
U.S. born (citizen)	69.5	85.1	20.6	75.2	29.7
Naturalized citizen	2.5	3.0	1.1	4.0	44.1
Non-citizen, residing <6 years	3.0	3.6	2.0	7.2	66.8
Non-citizen, residing at least 6 years	6.8	8.3	3.8	13.7	55.5

SOURCE: Hoffman and Pohl, 2000, Tables 7 and 8.

TABLE C.10 Distribution of the Uninsured Population Under Age 65 and Probabilities of Going Without Coverage, by Census Region of Residence, 1999

	No. in Population (<65 yrs) (millions)	% Distribution in Population	No. Uninsured (est.) (millions)	% Distribution Uninsured	% Uninsured Rate
By census region					
Totals	240.7	100.0	42.1	100.0	17.5
New England	11.9	4.9	1.4	3.3	11.6
Middle Atlantic	33.3	13.8	5.2	12.4	15.5
East North Central	39.7	16.5	5.3	12.6	13.3
West North Central	16.4	6.8	1.7	4.0	10.6
South Atlantic	42.2	17.5	7.9	18.8	18.8
East South Central	14.6	6.1	2.3	5.5	15.6
West South Central	26.8	11.1	6.5	15.4	24.4
Mountain	15.7	6.5	3.4	8.1	21.5
Pacific	40.2	16.7	8.5	20.2	21.1
By region					
Totals	238.6	100.0	42.7	100.0	17.9
Northeast	45.2	18.9	6.6	15.4	14.5
Midwest	55.9	23.4	8.0	18.7	14.4
South	82.5	34.6	16.4	38.4	19.9
West	54.9	23.0	11.6	27.1	21.1

SOURCES: Fronstin, 2000d, Table 7; Rhoades and Chu, 2000, Table 20.

TABLE C.11 Distribution of Uninsured Population Under Age 65 and Probabilities of Going Without Coverage, by State of Residence, 1997–1999

	No. in Population (<65 yrs) (millions)	% Distribution in Population	No. Uninsured (est.) (millions)	% Distribution Uninsured	% Uninsured Rate
U.S. total	238,504	100.0	43,056.0	100.0	18.1
Alabama	3,725	1.6	666.0	1.5	17.9
Alaska	587	0.2	115.0	0.3	19.6
Arizona	4,125	1.8	1,114.0	2.6	26.4
Arkansas	2,204	0.9	495.0	1.1	22.4
California	29,930	12.5	7,048.0	16.3	23.5
Colorado	3,654	1.5	628.0	1.5	17.2
Connecticut	2,856	1.2	376.0	0.9	13.2
Delaware	665	0.3	100.0	0.2	15.0
District of Columbia	442	0.2	81.0	0.2	18.4
Florida	12,055	5.0	2,726.0	6.3	22.6
Georgia	6,926	2.9	1,312.0	3.0	18.9
Hawaii	1,016	0.4	112.0	0.3	11.1
Idaho	1,118	0.5	229.0	0.5	20.4
Illinois	10,855	4.6	1,676.0	3.9	15.4
Indiana	5,188	2.2	712.0	1.6	13.7
Iowa	2,443	1.0	277.0	0.6	11.3
Kansas	2,229	0.9	297.0	0.7	13.3
Kentucky	3,419	1.4	565.0	1.3	16.5
Louisiana	3,775	1.6	866.0	2.0	23.0
Maine	1,092	0.4	163.0	0.4	14.9
Maryland	4,378	1.8	693.0	1.6	15.8
Massachusetts	5,317	2.2	669.0	1.5	12.6
Michigan	8,813	3.7	1,188.0	2.8	13.5
Minnesota	4,289	1.8	421.0	1.0	9.8
Mississippi	2,407	1.0	520.0	1.2	21.6

Missouri	4,704	2.0	568.0	1.3	12.1
Montana	798	0.3	174.0	0.4	21.8
Nebraska	1,463	0.6	170.0	0.4	11.6
Nevada	1,633	0.7	363.0	0.8	22.2
New Hampshire	1,093	0.4	135.0	0.3	12.4
New Jersey	7,106	3.0	1,219.0	2.8	17.2
New Mexico	1,596	0.7	418.0	1.0	26.2
New York	15,970	6.7	3,098.0	7.2	19.4
North Carolina	6,486	2.7	1,129.0	2.6	17.4
North Dakota	537	0.2	87.0	0.2	16.2
Ohio	9,826	4.1	1,227.0	2.8	12.5
Oklahoma	2,820	1.2	586.0	1.4	20.8
Oregon	2,979	1.2	470.0	1.1	15.8
Pennsylvania	10,189	4.3	1,181.0	2.7	11.6
Rhode Island	815	0.3	86.0	0.2	10.6
South Carolina	3,355	1.4	630.0	1.5	18.8
South Dakota	612	0.2	89.0	0.2	14.6
Tennessee	4,953	2.1	700.0	1.6	14.1
Texas	17,974	7.5	4,761.0	11.0	26.5
Utah	1,937	0.8	292.0	0.7	15.1
Vermont	528	0.2	62.0	0.1	11.8
Virginia	5,884	2.5	907.0	2.1	15.4
Washington	5,161	2.2	748.0	1.7	14.5
West Virginia	1,448	0.6	299.0	0.7	20.7
Wisconsin	4,610	1.9	531.0	1.2	11.5
Wyoming	430	0.2	78.0	0.2	18.2

SOURCE: Hoffman and Pohl, 2000, Tables 12 and 18.

TABLE C.12 Distribution of Uninsured Population Under Age 65 and Probabilities of Going Without Coverage, by Designation as Residing in Rural or Urban Areas, 1999

	No. in Population (<65 yrs) (millions)	% Distribution in Population	No. Uninsured (est.) (millions)	% Distribution Uninsured	% Uninsured Rate
By designation as metropolitan statistical area (MSA) or non-MSA					
Totals	238.6	100.0	42.5	100.0	17.8
Non-MSA	44.9	18.8	8.4	19.8	18.8
MSA	193.7	81.2	34.1	80.2	17.6

SOURCE: Rhoades and Chu, 2000, Tables 2 and 4.

TABLE C.13 Sources of Coverage (Percent) for Population Under Age 65, by Age Group, 1999

	Population	Adults	Children	Age (years)		
				<6	6-12	13-17
No insurance	17.5	19.1	13.9	13.9	13.4	14.5
Public insurance	14.2	10.4	22.9	26.9	22.8	18.4
Individually purchased	6.6	6.2	7.4	5.4	7.8	9.1
Employment-based	65.8	67.6	61.5	59.9	61.5	63.4
	Age (years)					
	18-24	25-34	35-44	45-54	55-64	
No insurance	24.0	23.3	16.6	13.4	14.5	
Public insurance	12.5	8.4	8.3	9.5	16.5	
Individually purchased	11.0	3.8	4.9	5.3	8.5	
Employment-based	51.1	66.7	72.5	75.1	67.0	

SOURCE: Fronstin, 2000d; Tables 1, 10, and 11.

TABLE C.14 Sources of Health Insurance (Percent) for Population Under Age 65, by Race and Ethnicity, 1999

	Population	Non-Hispanic White	Non-Hispanic African American	Hispanic	Other
No insurance	17.5	12.7	22.8	35.0	24.0
Public insurance	14.2	10.8	25.7	20.0	15.0
Individually purchased	6.6	7.5	4.2	4.2	6.0
Employment-based	65.8	72.8	53.1	44.0	59.1

SOURCE: Fronstin, 2000d, Table 6.

D

Multivariate Analyses

In the two tables that follow, the Committee reports estimates of how much uninsured rates may be influenced by specific socioeconomic, demographic, and geographic characteristics alone. These estimates were prepared for comparison with the uninsured rates presented in the body of this report. They were derived by means of multivariate statistical analysis, using data from the 2000 Current Population Survey (CPS) in the form of a derived variable file made available to the Committee by Paul Fronstin and the Employee Benefit Research Institute.[1] Four sets of analyses were performed to estimate and predict differences in uninsured rates by:

1. socioeconomic characteristics;
2. race and ethnicity;
3. immigrant and nativity status, both alone and specifically by race and ethnicity; and
4. geographic areas.

Tables D.1 and D.2 each present two sets of results for these analyses. The first column of each table reports comparisons of the likelihood of being uninsured between a group of interest and a reference group. For example, Hispanics are compared with non-Hispanic whites, with the difference in uninsured rate be-

---

[1]The Committee's analysis considers family units defined in terms of kin relationships, which may give different estimates than other analyses cited in this report, and based on CPS data, in which family units are defined in terms of insurance eligibility.

TABLE D.1 Estimated Independent Effects of Poverty Level, Education Level, Race and Ethnicity, and Immigrant and Nativity Status on Uninsured Rate

	Unadjusted Difference Between Uninsured Rate and Uninsured Rate for Reference Group (percentage points)	Predicted Difference if Coefficients (based on reference group's covariates) Were the Same as Those for the Reference Group (percentage points)
Effect of Poverty Level on Uninsured Rate (Reference Group: Families Earning >200% FPL)		
Families earning <100% FPL	24.2[a]	15.3[a]
Families earning 100–149% FPL	19.6[a]	12.4[a]
Families earning 150–199% FPL	15.8[a]	10.1[a]
Effect of Education Level on Uninsured rate (Reference Group: Primary Wage Earner with Postcollege Education)		
Primary wage earner has less than high school diploma	28.4[a]	16.2[a]
Primary wage earner has high school diploma	12.0[a]	7.9[a]
Primary wage earner has some college	8.2[a]	5.4[a]
Primary wage earner has college degree	2.2[a]	1.4[c]
Effect of Race and Ethnicity on Uninsured Rate (Reference Group: Non-Hispanic Whites)		
Non-Hispanic African American	10.0[a]	5.0[a]
Hispanic	22.2[a]	7.2[a]
All other groups	11.3[a]	5.4[a]
Effect of Immigrant and Nativity Status on Uninsured Rate (Reference Group: U.S. Born)		
All foreign-born persons		
Naturalized citizens	6.3[a]	2.5[a]
Long-term residents (at least 6 years)	16.9[a]	10.8[a]
Short-term residents (<6 years)	29.8[a]	14.8[a]
Foreign-born non-Hispanic whites (Reference Group: U.S. Born Non-Hispanic Whites)		
Naturalized citizens	0.7	0.7
Long-term residents (at least 6 years)	8.7[a]	6.9[b]
Short-term residents (<6 years)	13.8[a]	9.3[a]

TABLE D.1 Continued

	Unadjusted Difference Between Uninsured Rate and Uninsured Rate for Reference Group (percentage points)	Predicted Difference if Coefficients (based on reference group's covariates) Were the Same as Those for the Reference Group (percentage points)
Foreign-born non-Hispanic African Americans (Reference Group: U.S. Born Non-Hispanic African Americans)		
Naturalized citizens	7.6[a]	10.3[a]
Long-term residents		
(at least 6 years)	6.4	5.4
Short-term residents (<6 years)	18.7[a]	13.6[a]
Foreign-born Hispanics (Reference Group: U.S. Born Hispanics)		
Naturalized citizens	5.2[a]	5.5[a]
Long-term residents		
(at least 6 years)	15.8[a]	15.3[a]
Short-term residents (<6 years)	31.8[a]	21.0[a]

Notes: Effects are reported as follows: (1) the unadjusted uninsured rate, expressed in terms of the difference compared with the uninsured rate for the reference group; (2) the predicted uninsured rate, expressed in terms of the difference with the uninsured rate for the reference group, as adjusted for the covariates.

Models for poverty level and for education level include the following covariates: age, gender, nativity, race and ethnicity, whether urban or rural, family type, health status.

Model for race and ethnicity includes the following covariates: primary wage earner's education level, primary wage earner's work status, primary wage earner's occupation, whether primary wage earner has full-time or part-time job, size of firm employing primary wage earner (indicator), family income, age, gender, nativity, family type, state (indicator), whether urban or rural, health status.

Model for immigrant and nativity status includes the following covariates: primary wage earner's education level, primary wage earner's work status, primary wage earner's occupation, whether primary wage earner has full-time or part-time job, size of firm employing primary wage earner (indicator), family income, age, gender, family type, state (indicator), whether urban or rural, health status.

[a]$p < 0.01$
[b]$p < 0.05$
[c]$p < 0.10$

SOURCE: EBRI derived variable file, based on March 2000 Current Population Survey.

TABLE D.2 Estimated Independent Effect of State of Residence on Uninsured Rate

	Unadjusted Difference Between Uninsured Rate and National Average Uninsured Rate (17.5%) (percentage points)	Predicted Difference, if State's Covariates and Coefficients Were the Same as for National Averages (percentage points)
Alabama	−1.3	−1.2
Alaska	2.9[a]	4.3[a]
Arizona	6.8[a]	4.1[a]
Arkansas	−0.4	0.8
California	4.9[a]	−1.0[a]
Colorado	0.9	2.2[a]
Connecticut	−6.2[a]	−2.4[a]
Delaware	−4.6[a]	−2.7[a]
District of Columbia	0.1	−3.0[b]
Florida	5.4[a]	3.4[a]
Georgia	0.4	0.4
Hawaii	−5.0[a]	−8.3[a]
Idaho	4.1[a]	4.1[a]
Illinois	−1.8[a]	−0.5
Indiana	−5.2[a]	−2.2[a]
Iowa	−8.0[a]	−4.2[a]
Kansas	−3.5[a]	−1.4[c]
Kentucky	−1.0	1.0
Louisiana	7.6[a]	6.2[a]
Maine	−4.2[a]	−0.5
Maryland	−3.9[a]	−2.0[b]
Massachusetts	−5.7[a]	−4.6[a]
Michigan	−5.1[a]	−2.3[a]
Minnesota	−8.6[a]	−4.3[a]
Mississippi	1.5	1.2
Missouri	−7.9[a]	−4.1[a]
Montana	3.6[a]	2.8[a]
Nebraska	−5.2[a]	−2.2[a]
Nevada	5.3[a]	4.5[a]
New Hampshire	−6.2[a]	−2.0[b]
New Jersey	−2.5[a]	−1.0[c]
New Mexico	11.9[a]	7.4[a]
New York	1.0[b]	−1.1[a]
North Carolina	0.1	0.9
North Dakota	−3.5[a]	−1.4
Ohio	−5.0[a]	−1.6[a]
Oklahoma	3.0[a]	4.3[a]
Oregon	1.0	−0.6
Pennsylvania	−6.5[a]	−3.2[a]
Rhode Island	−9.4[a]	−6.2[a]
South Carolina	2.6[b]	4.6[a]
South Dakota	−3.9[a]	−0.9

TABLE D.2 Continued

	Unadjusted Difference Between Uninsured Rate and National Average Uninsured Rate (17.5%) (percentage points)	Predicted Difference, if State's Covariates and Coefficients Were the Same as for National Averages (percentage points)
Tennessee	−4.8[a]	−2.5[a]
Texas	8.3[a]	4.8[a]
Utah	−2.2[b]	1.3[c]
Vermont	−3.9[a]	−1.5
Virginia	−1.5	2.5[a]
Washington	0.1	2.4[a]
West Virginia	3.0[a]	4.1[a]
Wisconsin	−5.3[a]	−1.8[b]
Wyoming	0.6	2.7[a]

NOTES: Effects are reported as follows: (1) the unadjusted uninsured rate, expressed in terms of the difference compared with the uninsured rate for the reference group; (2) the predicted uninsured rate, expressed in terms of the difference with the uninsured rate for the reference group, as adjusted for the covariates

Model for state includes the following covariates: primary wage earner's education level, primary wage earner's work status, primary wage earner's occupation, whether primary wage earner has full-time or part-time job, size of firm employing primary wage earner (indicator), family income, age, gender, nativity, race and ethnicity, family type, state (indicator), whether urban or rural, health status.

[a] $p < 0.01$
[b] $p < 0.05$
[c] $p < 0.10$

SOURCE: EBRI derived variable file, based on March 2000 Current Population Survey.

tween the two groups reported in terms of percentage points. The second column reports a comparison between the same two groups as in the first column but taking into consideration, or adjusting for, population characteristics that are known to affect the likelihood of being uninsured and which often are closely related to, or highly correlated with, the group's identifying characteristic, for example, race and ethnicity.

For all four sets of comparisons, a series of logistic regression equations were prepared to estimate and predict uninsured rates, with the method of adjusting for population characteristics differing for each of the four sets of comparisons.[2]

---

[2]The Committee's analysis follows the method used by Ku and Matani, 2001, for using logistic regression models to estimate the probability of being uninsured, with comparisons between reference groups and comparison groups reported in terms of percentage point differences (in the case of Ku and Matani, in estimated mean change in the probability of having a specified source of coverage or being uninsured).

Except for the analysis of immigrant and nativity status, no interaction terms were used, on the assumption that change in the value of a measured characteristic (or covariate) is unlikely to lead to change in the values of other covariates in unique ways.

For the analyses by race and ethnicity, to arrive at the estimated difference reported in the second column of Table D.1, a logistic regression model was created to estimate the likelihood of being uninsured for the reference group and all comparison groups, taking into consideration or adjusting for all measured characteristics other than race and ethnicity.[3] This regression model also yielded a set of values, or coefficients, each of which describes the relative influence on the uninsured rate of a characteristic included in the model, for the reference group (e.g., non-Hispanic whites). To estimate the predicted differences reported in the second column of Table D.1, the same logistic regression model was used, combining the coefficients generated by the regression model for the reference group and the values (or covariate data) of the population characteristics (e.g., age, gender, health status) that describe the comparison group (e.g., non-Hispanic whites). The difference between this predicted likelihood of being uninsured (reported in column 2) and the reference group's estimated likelihood of being uninsured reflects differences between the comparison and reference group other than those reflected in the values for each population's measured characteristics.[4] Linear regression was used to evaluate the size and statistical significance of the difference (reported in column 2) between the predicted likelihood and the comparison group's estimated likelihood.[5] Because the results are presented in terms of differences between comparison and reference groups, an estimated uninsured rate of minus 1.1 percent, for example, is a rate that is 1.1 percentage points below the uninsured rate for the reference group.

For example, the logistic regression model based on population characteristics in our CPS data set gives an estimated uninsured rate for Hispanics that is 22.2 percentage points higher than the estimated uninsured rate for non-Hispanic

---

[3]The first step of the adjustment process included state fixed effects to control for state policy and other differences that would generate intra-state cluster effects.

[4]An alternative approach would be to prepare a single logistic regression with covariates for the characteristic of race and ethnicity and all other characteristics, plus interaction terms to describe the relationships between the characteristic of race and ethnicity and all of the other characteristics. Our adjusted comparison would consist of the difference in the probability predictions between what happens for the reference group and each of the comparison groups. This approach would require that the full model (including all covariates) be estimated for each subgroup, which is difficult given the size of some subgroups. The decision was made to limit the number of terms in the full model, because the main concern of the analysis is to evaluate the overall effect, or differences between estimated uninsured rates, rather than values of specific coefficients.

[5]The linear regression includes weights to account for differential sampling at each stage of the analysis.

whites, a difference that is statistically significant. If the differences in each population's measured characteristics influenced the likelihood of being uninsured in identical ways for both groups, and if there were no other influences on uninsured rates, the predicted difference between the uninsured rates for Hispanics and non-Hispanic whites should be zero. Instead, the predicted difference is 7.2 percentage points, a difference that is both statistically significantly different from zero and about 15 percentage points smaller than the unadjusted difference between the two groups. Therefore, two-thirds of the difference in estimated uninsured rates between Hispanics and non-Hispanic whites reflects differences in the values of measured population characteristics between these two groups, while approximately one-third of the difference reflects other factors that were not measured by the CPS data set or modeled in the multivariate analysis.

The analyses by immigrant and nativity status were similar to the analysis by race and ethnicity. For each group identified by race and ethnicity (e.g., Hispanic, non-Hispanic African American, and other), a logistic regression model was prepared to estimate an uninsured rate and a set of coefficients for a reference group of U.S. born citizens. The difference in estimated uninsured rates between each comparison group (e.g., foreign born, short-term resident, long-term resident) and the reference group is reported in column 1, stratified by race and ethnicity. To estimate the predicted differences in estimated uninsured rates reported in column 2, logistic regression models were prepared for each racial and ethnic group in which the coefficients for the reference group were combined with covariate data for each comparison group.[6] A preliminary analysis of the data suggested that stratifying the multivariate analysis by race and ethnicity would allow for the observation of important differences among populations of immigrants and naturalized citizens, especially useful for understanding uninsured rates within the Hispanic population.

The analyses by poverty level and education level of primary wage earner and the analysis by state were conducted using an approach that differed only slightly from the analysis by race and ethnicity. To obtain the estimated differences reported in the second column, a logistic regression model was created to estimate the likelihood of being uninsured for both the reference groups (e.g., families earning greater than 200 percent of the federal poverty level, and primary wage earner with postcollege education) and all comparison groups. This model took into account or adjusted for all the measured characteristics save for the characteristics of poverty level and education or state (in Table D.2). Linear regression analysis was used to evaluate the size and statistical significance of the difference (reported in column 2) between the adjusted likelihood of being uninsured for each comparison group and that of each reference group.[7]

---

[6]Linear regression was used to evaluate the adjusted comparison, with correction for oversampling and robust standard errors.

[7]For the linear regression analysis of the multivariate analyses by poverty and education and by state, weights were included to account for differential sampling.

The estimates reported in Tables D.1 and D.2 indicate that there is considerable variation, both in how much specific characteristics may influence a group's uninsured rate, independently of other measured characteristics, and in how much variation between uninsured rates is not accounted for by the measured characteristics used in the models. For example, the average uninsured rate for members of families earning less than 100 percent of FPL is estimated to be 24.2 percentage points higher than the average uninsured rate for members of families earning at least 200 percent of FPL. If members of families earning less than 100 percent of FPL as a group resembled members of families earning at least 200 percent of FPL, the uninsured rate for family members earning less than 100 percent of FPL would be predicted to be 15.3 percentage points, a 9 percentage-point or 37 percent diminution in the difference between uninsured rates. The 63 percent difference that remains cannot be attributed to differences in the measured characteristics (other than poverty level and education) and is not addressed by the models in this specific analysis. One would expect fairly large proportions of the differences in uninsured rates to remain unaccounted for by or associated with the specific characteristics evaluated, because there are many aspects of socioeconomic status, demographic characteristics, health status, and geography that are not measured in this analysis.

In every case, controlling for other correlated factors that influence insurance status reduces the estimated effect of a factor examined in the simple bivariate comparisons. In no case were the effects of those factors completely related to additional covariates.

E

Glossary

Access The timely use of personal health services to achieve the best possible health outcomes (Millman, 1993).

Adverse selection The disproportionate enrollment of individuals with poorer-than-average health expectations in certain health plans. Over time, as plan premiums rise as a result of higher enrollee health care costs, the plan becomes less attractive to relatively healthy potential enrollees, attracting relatively sicker enrollees disproportionately in successive enrollment cycles, which results in spiraling costs.

Ambulatory care-sensitive condition (ASC) Preventable or avoidable hospitalizations; a research construct used as an indicator of barriers to access to ambulatory care. Certain diagnoses for inpatient episodes are defined as preventable or avoidable if they are responsive to timely and appropriate ambulatory care. Rates of hospitalization above a specified baseline are construed as indicative of inadequate ambulatory care.

Benefit The particular services covered by a health plan and the amount payable for a loss under a specific insurance coverage (indemnity benefits) or as the guarantee of payment for certain services (service benefits).

Biased risk selection Exists (1) when individuals or groups that purchase insurance differ in their risk of incurring health care expenses from those who do not or (2) when those who enroll in competing health plans differ in the level of risk they present to different plans.

Catastrophic expense protection A health plan benefit that limits the amount the enrollee must pay out-of-pocket for coinsurance or other required cost sharing for covered services. Once the limit is reached, plans generally pay for any additional covered expenses in full for the remainder of the year or some other defined period.

Coinsurance The percentage of a covered medical expense that a beneficiary must pay (after any required deductible is met).

Community As used here, defined geographically, in terms of the residence of individuals and families or a political jurisdiction.

Community health center Also called a federally qualified health center (FQHC); a health services facility with a mandate and federal support to care for uninsured persons; when federally qualified, the center is authorized to receive cost-based reimbursement from the Medicare and Medicaid programs.

Community rating Setting health insurance premiums at the same level for all individuals or groups in a defined community. Modified community rating may set different rates for subgroups (e.g., individuals or small businesses or by age or gender).

Contingent worker One who works under conditions or arrangements different from full-time, full-year employment with a single employer, with the differences usually related to the time of work (hours and days of the week), the nonpermanent nature of the position, and the terms of the social contract (e.g., benefits) that usually bind employers and workers (Copeland et al., 1999).

Copayment A fixed payment per service (e.g., $15 per office visit or procedure) paid by a health plan member.

Core safety net providers Providers distinguished by two characteristics: (1) by legal mandate or explicitly adopted mission to maintain an "open door," access to services is offered for patients regardless of their ability to pay; and (2) a substantial share of the patient mix includes the uninsured, Medicaid recipients, and other vulnerable patients (Institute of Medicine, 2000).

Cost sharing The portion of health care expenses that a health plan member must pay directly, including deductibles, copayments, and coinsurance, but not including the premium.

Cost shifting Transfer of health care provider costs that are not reimbursed by one payer to other payers through higher charges for services.

Covered services Services eligible for payment by a health plan.

Creditable coverage In the context of health plan eligibility, prior health care coverage that is taken into account when determinng the allowable length of preexisting condition exclusion periods (for individuals entering group coverage) or when determining an individual's Health Insurance Portability and Accountability Act (HIPAA)-mandated eligibility when the individual is seeking individual nongroup coverage (adapted from HCFA, 2001).

Crowd-out A phenomenon whereby new public programs or expansions of existing public programs designed to extend coverage to the uninsured prompt some privately insured persons to drop their private coverage and take advantage of the expanded public subsidy.★

★From the Academy for Health Services Research and Health Policy glossary.

Deductible The amount of loss or expense that must be incurred by an insured or otherwise covered individual before an insurer will assume any liability for all or part of the remaining cost of covered services. Deductibles may be either fixed-dollar amounts or the value of specified services (such as two days of hospital care or one physician visit). Deductibles are usually tied to some reference period over which they must be incurred (e.g., $100 per calendar year, benefit period, or spell of illness.)★

Dependent An insured's spouse (not legally separated from the insured) and unmarried child(ren) who meet certain eligibility requirements and are not otherwise insured under the same group policy. The precise definition of a dependent varies by insurer or employer.

Exclusions Health care and related services (e.g., cosmetic surgery, long-term care) explicitly not covered by a health benefit plan.

Experience rating Basing health insurance premiums in whole or in part on the past claims history of a particular group or its anticipated future claims.

Federal poverty level (FPL) One of two federal poverty measurements; also known as "poverty guidelines." Issued annually in the *Federal Register* by the Department of Health and Human Services; it applies to persons of all ages in family units. The guidelines are a simplification of the poverty measurements for administrative purposes, for instance, determining financial eligibility for certain federal programs. In 1999, the FPL for a family unit of one was $8,240; for a family unit of three, $13,880; for a family unit of four, $16,700. In 2000 the FPL for a family unit of one, $8,350; for a family unit of three, $14,150; and for a family unit of four, $17,050. In 2001, the federal poverty level for a family unit of one, $8,590; for a family unit of three, $14,630; and for a family unit of four, $14,630. See Appendix C, Table C.1, for more information.

First-dollar coverage Health insurance requiring no deductible.

Full-year, full-time worker A person on full-time work schedule who works 35 hours or more per week, a person who worked 1–34 hours for noneconomic reason (e.g., illness) and usually works full-time, or someone "with a job but not at work" who usually works full-time.★

Full-year, part-time worker An individual who works at least 35 weeks during the year, works fewer than 35 hours in a typical week, and spends no time looking for work during the year.

Guaranteed issue Insurance coverage that does not require the insured to provide evidence of insurability.

Health care organization Entity that provides, coordinates, and/or insures health and medical services for people.

Health insurance Financial protection against the health care costs arising from disease, accidental bodily injury, or the direct provision of health care (as in some health maintenance organizations). Health insurance usually covers all or part of the costs of treating the disease or injury. Such insurance may be obtained on either an individual or a group basis. Charity care or direct provision by safety net providers is not considered a form of insurance coverage. Although the term is often used by policy makers to refer to comprehensive coverage, insurers and regulators also use it to refer to other forms of coverage such as long-term care insurance, supplemental insurance, specified disease policies, and accidental death and dismemberment insurance. ★

Health insurance premium An amount paid periodically to purchase health benefits. For self-insured groups that do not purchase insurance, the term may refer to the per-employee or per-family cost of health benefits and may be used for planning and analysis purposes even when no contribution to coverage is collected from the employee.

Health plan An organization or arrangement that provides defined medical expense protection (and sometimes medical services) to enrolled members.

High-risk pool Any arrangement established and maintained by a state primarily to provide health insurance benefits to certain state residents who, because of their poor health history, are unable to purchase individual coverage or can only acquire such coverage at a rate that is substantially above the rate offered by the high-risk pool. Coverage offered by a high-risk pool is comparable to individual coverage although sometimes at a higher price. The risk for that coverage is borne by the state, which generally supports the losses sustained by the pool through assessments on all health insurers doing business in the state, based on their relative market shares, and/or through general tax revenues.

Household An economic unit comprised of at least two persons, bound by a common residence but not necessarily by legal obligations.

Individual health insurance Health insurance purchased through an agent or an association formed for some other purpose, such as a professional organization.

Insurance Conventionally, the protection against significant, unpredictable financial loss from defined adverse events that is provided under written contract in return for payments (premiums) made in advance.

Job-lock A situation in which an employee is kept from changing jobs by fear of losing his or her health insurance, when changing jobs might otherwise be beneficial.

Loading factor The fraction added to the actuarial value of the covered benefit (i.e., to the expected or average amounts payable to the insured) to cover all additional administrative costs and contingencies of issuing the policy, including any profit for the insurer.

Managed care Term used broadly to describe health care plans that add utilization management features to indemnity-style coverage or, more narrowly, to identify group or network-based health plans that have explicit criteria for selecting providers and financial incentives for members to use network providers, who generally must cooperate with some form of utilization management. Managed care also includes a health plan that integrates the financing and delivery of services for covered individuals.

Medicaid The public health insurance program financed jointly by the federal government and the states, and administered by states, that covers certain categories of low-income individuals for health care services as required or permitted under Title XIX of the Social Security Act.

Medically underserved population A group experiencing a shortage of personal health services. A medically underserved population may or may not reside in a geographic area with a shortage of health professionals. Thus migrants, American Indians, or the inmates of a prison or mental hospital may constitute a medically underserved population. The term is defined and used to give priority for federal assistance through programs such as the National Health Services Corps.★

Medicare The federal health insurance program for people 65 years or older, certain people with disabilities, and people with permanent kidney failure treated with dialysis or a transplant. Medicare has two parts, hospital insurance (Part A) and supplemental medical insurance (Part B). It is authorized by Title XVIII of the Social Security Act. Part A is financed by payroll taxes and Part B by a combination of enrollee premium payments and general revenues.

Near-elderly or **midlife adult** Working-age adult within a decade of reaching the age of 65 years and becoming eligible for Medicare (age 55 through 64 years).

Out-of-pocket expenses Payments made by a plan enrollee for medical services that are not reimbursed by the health plan. Out-of-pocket expenses can include payments for deductibles, coinsurance, services not covered by the plan, provider charges in excess of the plan's limits, and enrollee premium payments.

Portability of benefits A guarantee of continuous coverage without waiting periods (e.g., for a preexisting health condition) for persons moving between plans.★

Preexisting condition A physical or mental condition that exists prior to the effective date of health insurance coverage.

Primary care The provision of integrated, accessible health care services by clinicians who are accountable for addressing a large majority of personal health care needs, developing a sustained partnership with patients, and practicing in the context of family and community (Institute of Medicine, 1996).

Quality of care Degree to which health services for individuals and populations increase the likelihood of desired health outcomes and are consistent with current professional knowledge (IOM, 1990).

Risk The chance of loss. In health insurance, risks relate to the chance of health care expenses arising from illness or injury and the responsibility for paying for or otherwise providing a level of health care services based on an unpredictable need for these services. ★

Safety net Term referring to those providers that organize and deliver a significant level of health care and other related services to uninsured, Medicaid, and other at-risk, lower-income patients (Institute of Medicine, 2000).

Self-insurance Funding of medical care expenses, generally by an employer, in whole or part through internal resources rather than through transfer of risk to an insurer.

Social insurance Old-age, disability, health, or other insurance that is mandated by statute for defined categories of individuals or the entire population, usually financed by payroll and other taxes.

Take-up rate The ratio of employees who enroll in a health insurance plan to those who are eligible to enroll.

Third-party payer An organization other than the patient (first party) or health care provider (second party) involved in the financing of personal health care services.

Uncompensated care Health care rendered to persons unable to pay and not covered by private or government health insurance plans; includes both unbilled charity care and bad debts (services billed but not paid).

Underinsured Individual and family situations in which the health insurance policy or health benefits plan is less than complete and comprehensive. For example, the family may lack coverage for specific services, have a maximum benefits limit or cap on covered services, or have a high copayment or coinsurance rates.

Underwriting An insurance practice of determining whether to accept or refuse individuals or groups for insurance coverage (or to adjust coverage or premiums) on the basis of an assessment of the risk they pose and other criteria (e.g., insurer's business objectives).

Uninsurance The individual or collective status of lacking health insurance coverage.

F

Biographical Sketches

Mary Sue Coleman, Ph.D., *Co-chair,* is president of the University of Iowa and president of the University of Iowa Health Systems. She holds academic appointments as professor of biochemistry in the College of Medicine and professor of biological sciences in the College of Liberal Arts. Dr. Coleman served as provost and vice president for academic affairs at the University of New Mexico (1993–1995) and as dean of research and vice chancellor at the University of North Carolina at Chapel Hill (1990–1992). She was both faculty member and administrator of the Cancer Center at the University of Kentucky in Lexington for 19 years, where her research focused on the immune system and malignancies. Dr. Coleman is a member of the Institute of Medicine (IOM), the American Academy of Arts and Sciences, and a fellow of the American Association for the Advancement of Science. She has served on the Iowa Governor's Strategic Planning Council, the Board of Trustees of the Universities Research Association, the Board of Governors of the Warren G. Magnuson Clinical Center at the National Institutes of Health, and other voluntary advisory bodies and corporate boards.

Arthur L. Kellermann, M.D., M.P.H., *Co-chair,* is professor and director, Center for Injury Control, Rollins School of Public Health, Emory University, and professor and chairman, Department of Emergency Medicine, School of Medicine, Emory University. Dr. Kellermann has served as principal investigator or coinvestigator on several research grants, including federally funded studies of handgun-related violence and injury, emergency cardiac care, and the use of emergency room services. Among his many awards and distinctions, he is a fellow of the American College of Emergency Physicians (1992), is the recipient of a meritorious service award from the Tennessee State Legislature (1993) and the Hal

Jayne Academic Excellence Award from the Society for Academic Emergency Medicine (1997), and was elected to membership of the Institute of Medicine in 1999. In addition, Dr. Kellermann is a member of the Editorial Board of the journal *Annals of Emergency Medicine* and has served as a reviewer for the *New England Journal of Medicine*, the *Journal of the American Medical Association*, and the *American Journal of Public Health*.

Ronald M. Andersen, Ph.D. is the Fred W. and Pamela K. Wasserman Professor of Health Services and professor of sociology at the University of California, Los Angeles School of Public Health. He teaches courses in health services organization, research methods, evaluation, and leadership. Dr. Andersen received his Ph.D. in sociology at Purdue University. He has studied access to medical care for his entire professional career of 30 years. Dr. Andersen developed the Behavioral Model of Health Services Use that has been used extensively nationally and internationally as a framework for utilization and cost studies of general populations as well as special studies of minorities, low-income populations, children, women, the elderly, oral health, the homeless, and the HIV-positive population. He has directed three national surveys of access to care and has led numerous evaluations of local and regional populations and programs designed to promote access to medical care. Dr. Andersen's other research interests include international comparisons of health services systems, graduate medical education curricula, physician health services organization integration, and evaluations of geriatric and primary care delivery. He is a member of the IOM and was on the founding board of the Association for Health Services Research. He has been chair of the Medical Sociology Section of the American Sociological Association. In 1994 he received the Association's Leo G. Reeder Award for Distinguished Service to Medical Sociology; in 1996, he received the Distinguished Investigator Award from the Association for Health Services Research; and in 1999, he received the Baxter Allegiance Health Services Research Prize.

John Z. Ayanian, M.D., M.P.P.,[*] is an associate professor of medicine and health care policy at Harvard Medical School and Brigham and Women's Hospital, where he practices general internal medicine. His research focuses on quality of care and access to care for major medical conditions, including colorectal cancer and myocardial infarction. He has extensive experience in the use of cancer registries to assess outcomes and evaluate the quality of cancer care. In addition, he has studied the effects of race and gender on access to kidney transplants and on quality of care for other medical conditions. Dr. Ayanian is deputy editor of the journal *Medical Care*, a Robert Wood Johnson Foundation Generalist Physician Faculty Scholar, and a fellow of the American College of Physicians.

---

[*] Member of the Subcommittee on the Status of the Uninsured.

Robert J. Blendon, M.B.A., Sc.D., is currently professor of health policy and political analysis at both the Harvard School of Public Health and the John F. Kennedy School of Government and has received outstanding teaching awards from both institutions. He also directs the Harvard Opinion Research Program and the Henry J. Kaiser National Program on Public Opinion and Health and Social Policy, which focuses on better understanding of public knowledge, attitudes, and beliefs about major domestic public policy issues. Dr. Blendon also codirects the *Washington Post*–Kaiser Family Foundation (KFF) survey project, which was nominated for a Pulitzer Prize, and a new project for National Public Radio and KFF on American attitudes toward health and social policy, which was cited by the *National Journal* as setting a new standard of public opinion surveys in broadcast journalism. From 1987 to 1996, Dr. Blendon served as chair of the Department of Health Policy and Management at the Harvard School of Public Health and as deputy director of the Harvard University Division of Health Policy Research and Education. Prior to his Harvard appointment, Dr. Blendon was senior vice president at The Robert Wood Johnson Foundation. He was senior editor of a three volume series *The Future of American Health Care* and is a member of the IOM, the advisory committee to the director of the Centers for Disease Control and Prevention, and the editorial board of the *Journal of the American Medical Association*. Dr. Blendon is a graduate of Marietta College and received his master's of business administration and doctoral degrees from the University of Chicago and the Johns Hopkins School of Public Health, respectively.

Peter Cunningham, Ph.D.,★ is a senior health researcher at the Center for Studying Health System Change, where he has been involved extensively with the design and analysis of the Community Tracking Study. He has had primary responsibility for overseeing the design and implementation of the Community Tracking Study household survey and the followback survey to health insurance plans. In terms of his research, Dr. Cunningham has been concerned primarily with the uninsured, specifically in understanding variations across communities in uninsurance rates, access to care for uninsured persons, and the role of the health care safety net. Prior to joining the center in April 1995, Dr. Cunningham was a researcher at the Agency for Health Care Policy and Research (now the Agency for Healthcare Research and Quality [AHRQ]), where he worked on the 1987 National Medical Expenditure Survey, including the Household Survey, the Survey of American Indians and Alaska Natives, and the Institutional Population Component. Dr. Cunningham's research focused on issues concerning health insurance coverage, access to care, health care utilization and expenditures for children, people eligible for the Indian Health Service, poor and low-income people, and other disadvantaged groups. Dr. Cunningham holds a Ph.D. and a master's in Sociology from Purdue University.

Sheila P. Davis, B.S.N., M.S.N., Ph.D.,★ is associate professor, Department of Adult Health, in the School of Nursing at the University of Mississippi Medical

Center. She is also vice president of Davis, Davis & Associates, a health management consultant company. Her research focuses on minority health issues, especially cardiovascular risk among ethnic populations. Dr. Davis is the founder and chair of the Cardiovascular Risk Reduction in Children Committee at the University of Mississippi. This is a multidisciplinary committee (physicians, nurses, dietician, health educator, college administrator, nurse practitioners, etc.) committed to reducing cardiovascular risks in children. Dr. Davis is a member of the American Nurses Association and has written numerous publications on the profession and the experiences of ethnic minorities in the health professions. She is author of a faith-based program, Healthy Kids Seminar, which is used to promote the adoption of healthy life-style choices by children.

George C. Eads, Ph.D. is vice president and director of the Washington, D.C. office of Charles River Associates (CRA) and is an internationally known expert in the economics of the automotive and airlines industries. Prior to joining CRA, Dr. Eads was vice president and chief economist at General Motors Corporation. He frequently represented the corporation before congressional committees and federal regulatory agencies. He has served as a member of the President's Council of Economic Advisers and as a special assistant to the assistant attorney general in the Antitrust Division of the U.S. Department of Justice. Dr. Eads has published numerous books and articles on the impact of government on business and has taught at several major universities, including Harvard and Princeton.

Paul Fronstin, Ph.D.,★ is a senior research associate with the Employee Benefit Research Institute (EBRI). He is also director of EBRI's Health Security and Quality Research Program. Dr. Fronstin's research interests include trends in health insurance coverage and the uninsured, the effectiveness of managed care, retiree health benefits, retirement transitions, employee benefits and taxation, the role of nonprofit organizations in providing employee benefits, children's health insurance coverage, and public opinion about health care. His most recent publications include papers in the *Gerontologist, Journal of Health Politics, Policy and Law,* and *Health Affairs.*

Sandra R. Hernández, M.D., is the chief executive officer (CEO) of The San Francisco Foundation, a community foundation serving the five Bay Area counties. It is one of the largest community foundations in the country. Dr. Hernández is a primary care internist who previously held a number of positions within the San Francisco Department of Public Health, including director of the AIDS Office, director of community public health, county health officer, and finally director of health for the City and County of San Francisco. She was appointed to and served on President Clinton's Advisory Commission on Consumer Protection and Quality in the Healthcare Industry. Among the many honors and awards bestowed on her, Dr. Hernández was named by *Modern Healthcare* magazine as one of the top ten health care leaders for the next century. Dr. Hernández is a graduate of Yale University, Tufts School of Medicine, and the JFK School of Government at Harvard University. She is on the faculty of University of California, San Francisco (UCSF) School of Medicine and maintains an active clinical practice at San Francisco General Hospital in the AIDS Clinic.

Catherine Hoffman, Sc.D., R.N.,★ is an associate director of the Kaiser Commission on Medicaid and the Uninsured. She has focused her health services research career on differences in access to health care, particularly for vulnerable populations including low-income families, the uninsured, and those with chronic health problems. Dr. Hoffman has held both research and analytical positions in several organizations including the Institute for Health and Aging at UCSF, the Physician Payment Review Commission, and Kaiser Commission on the Future of Medicaid. She received her doctoral degree in health policy and management from the Johns Hopkins University School of Hygiene and Public Health and builds her health policy career on a clinical foundation as a nurse specialist in cardiac care.

Willard G. Manning, Ph.D.,★ is professor in the Department of Health Studies, Pritzker School of Medicine, and in the Harris School of Public Policy at the University of Chicago. His primary research focus has been on the effects of health insurance and alternative delivery systems on the use of health services and health status. He is an expert in statistical issues in cost-effectiveness analysis and small-area variations. His recent work has included examination of mental health services use and outcomes in a Medicaid population and cost-effectiveness analysis of screening and treating depression in primary care. Dr. Manning is a member of the Institute of Medicine.

James J. Mongan, M.D., is president and COO of Massachusetts General Hospital. He was previously executive director, Truman Medical Center and dean, University of Missouri-Kansas City School of Medicine. Dr. Mongan served as assistant surgeon general in the Department of Health and Human Services as former associate director for health and human resources, Domestic Policy Staff, the White House, and as former deputy assistant secretary for health policy, Department of Health, Education and Welfare. Dr. Mongan is chair of the Task Force on the Future of Health Insurance for Working Americans, a nonpartisan effort of the Commonwealth Fund to address the implications of the changing United States work force and economy for the availability and affordability of health insurance, and is a member of the Kaiser Family Foundation Board and the Kaiser Commission on Medicaid and the Uninsured. Dr. Mongan is a member of the Institute of Medicine.

Christopher Queram, M.H.S.A., has been CEO of the Employer Health Care Alliance Cooperative (The Alliance) of Madison, Wisconsin, since 1993. The Alliance is a purchasing cooperative owned by more than 175 member companies that contracts with providers, manages and reports data, performs consumer education, and designs employer and provider quality initiatives. Prior to his current position, Mr. Queram served as vice president for Programs at Meriter Hospital, a 475-bed hospital in Madison. Mr. Queram is a member of the Board of the National Business Coalition on Health and served as board chair for the past two years. He was a member of the President's Advisory Commission on Consumer Protection and Quality in the Health Care Industry. Mr. Queram served as a member of the Planning Committee for the National Quality Forum and continues as convenor of the Purchaser Council of the Forum. He is a member of the Wisconsin Board on Health Information and the Board of the Wisconsin Private Employer Health Care Coverage program. He holds a master's degree in health services administration from the University of Wisconsin at Madison and is a fellow in the American College of Healthcare Executives.

Shoshanna Sofaer, Dr.P.H., is the Robert P. Luciano Professor of Health Care Policy at the School of Public Affairs, Baruch College, in New York City. She completed her master's and doctoral degrees in public health at the University of California, Berkeley, taught for six years at the University of California, Los Angeles School of Public Health, and served on the faculty of George Washington University Medical Center, where she was professor, associate dean for research of the School of Public Health and Health Services, and director of the Center for Health Outcomes Improvement Research. Dr. Sofaer's research interests include providing information to individual consumers on the performance of the health care system; assessing the impact of information on both consumers and the system; developing consumer-relevant performance measures; and improving the responsiveness of the Medicare program to the needs of current and future cohorts of older persons and persons with disabilities. In addition, Dr. Sofaer studies the role of community coalitions in pursuing public health and health care system reform objectives, and has extensive experience in the evaluation of community health improvement interventions. She has studied the determinants of health insurance status among the near-elderly, including early retirees. Dr. Sofaer served as co-chair of the Working Group on Coverage for Low Income and Non-Working Families for the White House Task Force on Health Care Reform in 1993. Currently, she is co-chair of the Task Force on Medicare of the Century Foundation in New York City, a member of the IOM Board on Health Care Services, and a member of the AHRQ Health Systems Study Section.

Stephen J. Trejo, Ph.D., is associate professor in the Department of Economics at the University of Texas at Austin. His primary research focus has been in the field of labor economics. He has examined the response of labor market participants to the incentives created by market opportunities, government policies, and the institutional environment. Specific research topics include the economic effects of overtime pay regulation; immigrant labor market outcomes and welfare recipiency; the impact of labor unions on compensation, employment, and work schedules; the importance of sector-specific skills; and the relative economic status of Mexican Americans.

Reed V. Tuckson, M.D., is senior vice president of consumer health and medical care enhancement at United Health Group. Formerly, he was senior vice president, professional standards at the American Medical Association. Dr. Tuckson was president of Charles R. Drew University School of Medicine and Science from 1991 to 1997. From 1986 to 1990, he was commissioner of public health for the District of Columbia. Dr. Tuckson serves on a number of health care, academic, and federal boards and committees and is a nationally known lecturer on topics concerning community-based medicine, the moral responsibilities of health professionals, and physician leadership. He currently serves on the IOM Roundtable on Research and Development of Drugs, Biologics, and Medical Devices and is a member of the Institute of Medicine.

Edward H. Wagner, M.D., M.P.H., F.A.C.P., is a general internist–epidemiologist and director of the W.A. MacColl Institute for Healthcare Innovation at the Center for Health Studies, Group Health Cooperative of Puget Sound. He is also professor of health services at the University of Washington School of Public Health and Community Medicine. Current research interests include the development and testing of population-based care models for diabetes, the frail elderly, and chronic illnesses; the evaluation of the health and cost impacts of chronic disease and cancer interventions; and interventions to prevent disability and reduce depressive symptoms in older adults. Dr. Wagner has written two books and more than 200 journal articles. He serves on the editorial boards of *Health Services Research* and the *Journal of Clinical Epidemiology* and acts as a consultant to multiple federal agencies and private foundations. He recently completed a stint as senior adviser on managed care initiatives in the director's office of the National Institutes of Health. As of June 1998, he directs Improving Chronic Illness Care (ICIC), a national program of The Robert Wood Johnson Foundation. The overall goal of ICIC is to assist health systems improve their care of chronic illness through quality improvement and evaluation, research, and dissemination. Dr. Wagner is also Principal Investigator of the Cancer Research Network, a National Cancer Institute funded consortium of ten health maintenance organizations conducting collaborative cancer effectiveness research.

Lawrence Wallack, Dr.P.H.,★ is professor of public health and director, School of Community Health at Portland State University. He is also professor of public health, University of California, Berkeley. Dr. Wallack's primary interest is in the role of mass communication, particularly the news media, in shaping public health issues. His current research is focused on how public health issues are framed in print and broadcast news. He is principal author of *Media Advocacy and Public Health: Power for Prevention and News for a Change: An Advocate's Guide to Working with the Media.* He is also coeditor of *Mass Communications and Public Health:*

Complexities and Conflicts. Dr. Wallack has published extensively on topics related to prevention, health promotion, and community interventions. Specific content areas of his research and intervention work have included alcohol, tobacco, violence, handguns, sexually transmitted diseases, cervical and breast cancer, affirmative action, suicide, and childhood lead poisoning. Dr. Wallack is a member of the IOM Committee on Communication for Behavior Change in the 21st Century: Improving the Health of Diverse Populations.

References

Academy for Health Services Research and Health Policy. 2000. *Glossary of Terms Commonly Used in Health Care.* Accessed January 24, 2001. Available at http://academyhealth.org/publications/glossary.pdf.

Acs, Gregory, and Linda J. Blumberg. 2001. How a Changing Workforce Affects Employer-Sponsored Health Insurance. *Health Affairs* 20(1):178–183.

Acs, Gregory, and John Sabelhaus. 1995. Trends in Out-Of-Pocket Spending on Health Care, 1980–92. *Monthly Labor Review* 118:35–45.

Acs, Gregory, Stephen H. Long, M. Susan Marquis, and Pamela Farley Short. 1996. Self-Insured Employer Health Plans: Prevalence, Profile, Provisions, and Premiums. *Health Affairs* 15(2):266–278.

Aday, Lu Ann, G.V. Fleming, and Ronald Andersen. 1984. *Access to Medical Care in the U.S.: Who Has It, Who Doesn't.* Chicago, IL: Pluribus Press.

Agency for Healthcare Research and Quality. Center for Cost and Financing Studies. 2001. Unpublished data from 1999 MEPS.

Alteras, Tanya T. 2001. *Understanding the Dynamics of "Crowd-Out": Defining Public/Private Coverage Substitution for Policy and Research.* Washington, DC: Academy for Health Services Research and Health Policy, Changes in Health Care Financing and Organization Program. Accessed June 19, 2001. Available at http://www.hcfo.net/

Andersen, Ronald M. 1995. Revisiting the Behavioral Model and Access to Medical Care: Does It Matter? *Journal of Health and Social Behavior* 36:1–10.

Andersen, Ronald M., and Lu Ann Aday. 1978. Access to Medical Care in the U.S.: Realized and Potential. *Medical Care* 16:533–546.

Andersen, Ronald, and Odin W. Anderson. 1999. National Medical Expenditure Surveys. Genesis and Rationale. In: Alan C. Monheit, Renate Wilson, and Ross H. Arnett III, (eds.) *Informing American Health Care Policy. The Dynamics of Medical Expenditure and Insurance Surveys, 1977–1996.* San Francisco, CA: Jossey-Bass. Pp. 11–30.

Andersen, Ronald M., and Pamela Davidson. 2001. Improving Access to Care in America: Individual and Contextual Indicators. In: Ronald Andersen, Thomas Rice, and Gerald Kominski (eds.) *Changing the U.S. Health Care System: Key Issues in Health Services, Policy and Management,* San Francisco, CA: Jossey-Bass. Pp. 3–30.

Ayanian, John Z., Joel S. Weissman, Eric C. Schneider, Jack A. Ginsburg, and Alan M. Zaslavsky. 2000. Unmet Health Needs of Uninsured Adults in the United States. *Journal of the American Medical Association* 284(16):2061–2069.

Ayanian, John Z., Betsy A. Kohler, Toshi Abe, et al. 1993. The Relation Between Health Insurance Coverage and Clinical Outcomes Among Women with Breast Cancer. *New England Journal of Medicine* 329(5):326–331.

Baker, David W., Martin F. Shapiro, and Claudia L. Schur. 2000. Health Insurance and Access to Care for Symptomatic Conditions. *Archives of Internal Medicine* 160(9):1269–1274.

Baker, David W., Carl D. Stevens, and Robert H. Brook. 1994. Regular Source of Ambulatory Care and Medical Care Utilization by Patients Presenting to a Public Hospital Emergency Department. *Journal of the American Medical Association* 271(24):1909–1912.

Banja, John D. 2000. The Improbable Future of Employment-Based Insurance. *Hastings Center Report* 30(3):17–25.

Bennefield, Robert. 1998a. Dynamics of Economic Well-Being: Health Insurance, 1993 to 1995. Who Loses Coverage and for How Long? *Census Bureau Current Population Reports. Household Economic Studies*, P70–64. Washington, DC: U.S. Census Bureau.

————. 1998b. Health Insurance Coverage: 1997. *Census Bureau Current Population Reports. Household Economic Studies*. P60–202:1–7. Washington, DC: U.S. Census Bureau.

Berk, M.L., and A.C. Monheit. 2001. The Concentration of Health Care Expenditures, Revisited. *Health Affairs* 20(2):9–18.

Berk, Marc L., Claudia L. Schur, Leo R. Chavez, and Martin Frankel. 2000. Health Care Use Among Undocumented Latino Immigrants. *Health Affairs* 19(4):51–64.

Bernstein, Jared, Chauna Brocht, and Maggie Spade-Aguilar. 2000. *How Much Is Enough?* Washington, DC: Economic Policy Institute.

Bilheimer, Linda T., and David C. Colby. 2001. Expanding Coverage: Reflections on Recent Efforts. *Health Affairs* 20(1):83–95.

Bindman, Andrew B., Kevid Grumbach, Dennis Osmand, et al. 1995. Preventable Hospitalizations and Access to Care. *Journal of the American Medical Association* 274(4):305–311.

Blendon, Robert J., John T. Young, and Catherine M. DesRoches. 1999. The Uninsured, the Working Uninsured, and the Public. *Health Affairs* 18(6):203–211.

Blue Cross Blue Shield Association. 2000. *State Legislative Health Care and Insurance Issues: 2000 Survey of Plans*. Washington, D.C.: Blue Cross–Blue Shield Association.

Blumberg, Linda J. 1999. Who Pays For Employer-Sponsored Health Insurance? *Health Affairs* 18(6):58–61.

Brennan, Niall. 2000. Health Insurance Coverage of the Near-Elderly. No. B21. Washington, DC: The Urban Institute.

Broaddus, Matthew, and Leighton Ku. 2000. Nearly 95 Percent of Low-Income Uninsured Children Now Are Eligible for Medicaid or SCHIP. Washington, DC: Center on Budget and Policy Priorities. Accessed May 7, 2001. Available at http://www.cbpp.org.

Brown, E. Richard, Victoria D. Ojeda, Roberta Wyn, and Rebecka Levan. 2000a. *Racial and Ethnic Disparities in Access to Health Insurance and Health Care*. Los Angeles, CA: UCLA Center for Health Policy Research.

Brown, E. Richard, Roberta Wyn, and Stephanie Teleki. 2000b. *Disparities in Health Insurance and Access to Care for Residents Across U.S. Cities*. Los Angeles, CA: UCLA Center for Health Policy Research.

————. 2000c. *Disparities in Health Insurance and Access to Care Of Residents Across U.S. Cities Supplement: Data From 85 Metropolitan Statistical Areas*. Los Angeles, CA: UCLA Center for Health Policy Research.

Brown, E. Richard, Ninez Ponce, and Thomas Rice. 2001. *The State of Health Insurance in California: Recent Trends, Future Prospects*. Los Angeles, CA: UCLA Center for Health Policy Research.

Brown, E. Richard, Roberta Wyn, Hongjian Yu, Abel Valenzuela, et al. 1999. Access to Health Insurance and Health Care for Children in Immigrant Families. In: Donald J Hernandez (ed.). Committee on the Health and Adjustment of Immigrant Children and Families, *Children of Immigrants. Health, Adjustment, and Public Assistance.* Washington, DC: National Academy Press. Pp. 126–186.

Brown, Margaret E., Andrew B. Bindman, and Nicole Lurie. 1998. Monitoring the Consequences of Uninsurance: A Review of the Methodologies. *Medical Care Research and Review* 55(2):177–210.

Buchmueller, Thomas C. 1996–1997. Marital Status, Spousal Coverage, and the Gender Gap in Employer-Sponsored Health Insurance. *Inquiry* 33:308–316.

Budetti, John, Duchon, Lisa, Schoen, Cathy, and Janet Shikles. 1999. *Can't Afford to Get Sick: A Reality for Millions of Working Americans.* New York: Commonwealth Fund.

Burstin, Helen R., Katherine Swartz, Anne C. O'Neill, et al. 1998. The Effect of Change of Health Insurance on Access to Care. *Inquiry* 35:389–397.

Camarota, Steven A., and James R. Edwards, Jr. 2000. *Without Coverage. Immigration's Impact on the Size and Growth of the Population Lacking Health Insurance.* Washington, DC: Cener for Immigration Studies. Accessed May 7, 2001. Available at http://www.cis.org.

Carrasquillo, Olveen, David U. Himmelstein, Steffie Woolhandler, and David H. Bor. 1998. Can Medicaid Managed Care Provide Continuity of Care to New Medicaid Enrollees? An Analysis of Tenure on Medicaid. *American Journal of Public Health* 88(3):464–466.

Carrasquillo, Olveen, Angeles I. Carrasquillo, and Steven Shea. 2000. Health Insurance Coverage of Immigrants Living in the United States: Differences by Citizenship Status and Country of Origin. *American Journal of Public Health* 90(6):917–923.

Carrasquillo, Olveen, David U. Himmelstein, Steffie Woolhandler, and David H. Bor. 1999a. Going Bare: Trends in Health Insurance Coverage, 1989 Through 1996. *American Journal of Public Health* 89(1):36–42.

———. 1999b. A Reappraisal of Private Employers' Role in Providing Health Insurance. *New England Journal of Medicine* 340(2):109–114.

Chernew, Michael, Kevin Frick, and Catherine McLaughlin. 1997. The Demand for Health Insurance Coverage by Low-Income Workers: Can Reduced Premiums Achieve Full Coverage? *Health Services Research* 32(4):453–470.

Chollet, Deborah J. 2000. Consumers, Insurers, and Market Behavior. *Journal of Health Politics, Policy and Law* 25(1):27–44.

Chollet, Deborah J., Adele M. Kirk, and Marc E. Chow. 2000. *Mapping State Health Insurance Markets: Structure and Change in the States' Group and Individual Health Insurance Markets, 1995–1997.* Washington, DC: Academy for Health Services Research and Health Policy, State Coverage Initiative. Accessed July 2, 2001. Available at http://www.academyhealth.org/.

Chollet, Deborah, and Adele Kirk. 1998. *Understanding Individual Health Insurance Markets: Structure, Practices, and Products in Ten States.* Menlo Park, CA: The Henry J. Kaiser Family Foundation.

Coburn, Andrew F., Elizabeth H. Kilbreth, Stephen H. Long, and M. Susan Marquis. 1998. Urban–Rural Differences in Employer-Based Health Insurance Coverage of Workers. *Medical Care Research and Review* 55(4):484–496.

Cooper, Philip F., and Barbara Steinberg Schone. 1997. More Offers, Fewer Takers for Employment Based Health Insurance: 1987 and 1996. *Health Affairs* 16(6):142–149.

Copeland, Craig. 1998. Characteristics of the Nonelderly with Selected Sources of Health Insurance and Lengths of Uninsured Spells. *Issue Brief 198.* Washington, DC: Employee Benefit Research Institute.

Copeland, Craig, Paul Fronstin, Pamela Ostua, and Paul Yakoboski. 1999. Contingent Workers and Workers in Alternative Work Arrangements. *Issue Brief No. 207.* Washington, DC: Employee Benefit Research Institute.

Culyer, Anthony J. and Joseph P. Newhouse (eds.). 2000. *Handbook of Health Economics.* New York: Elsevier.

Cunningham, Peter J. 1999a. *Choosing to Be Uninsured: Determinants and Consequences of the Decision to Decline Employer-Sponsored Health Insurance.* Washington, DC: Center for Studying Health System Change.

———. 1999b. Pressures on Safety Net Access: The Level of Managed Care Penetration and Uninsurance Rate in a Community. *Health Services Research* 34(1):255–270.

Cunningham, Peter, and Paul B. Ginsburg. 2001. What Accounts for Differences in Uninsurance Rates Across Communities? *Inquiry* 38(10):6-21.

Cunningham, Peter J., and Ha T. Tu. 1997. A Changing Picture of Uncompensated Care. *Health Affairs* 14(4):167–175.

Cunningham, Peter J., and Peter Kemper. 1998. Ability to Obtain Medical Care for the Uninsured. How Much Does It Vary Across Communities? *Journal of the American Medical Association* 280(10):921–927.

Cunningham, Peter J., and Michael H. Park. 2000. *Recent Trends in Children's Health Insurance Coverage: No Gains for Low-Income Children.* Issue Brief No. 29. Findings from HSC. Washington, DC: Center for Studying Health System Change. Accessed May 7, 2001. Available at http://www.hschange.org.

Cunningham, Peter J., and Heidi Whitmore. 1998. *How Well Do Communities Perform on Access to Care for the Uninsured?* Washington, DC: Center for Studying Health System Change.

Cunningham, Peter, Elizabeth Schaefer, and Christopher Hogan. 1999a. *Who Declines Employer-Sponsored Health Insurance and Is Uninsured?* Issue Brief No. 22. Findings from HSC. Washington, DC: Center for Studying Health System.

Cunningham, Peter J., Joy M. Grossman, Robert F. St. Peter, et al. 1999c. Managed Care and Physicians' Provision of Charity Care. *Journal of the American Medical Association* 281(12):1087–1092.

Currie, Janet, and Brigitte C. Madrian. 1999. Health, Health Insurance, and the Labor Market. In: Orley Ashenfelter and David Card (eds.) *Handbook of Labor Economics, Vol. 3.* New York: North-Holland. Pp. 3309–3415.

Custer, William S., and Pat Ketsche. 2000a. *The Changing Sources of Health Insurance.* Washington, DC: Health Insurance Association of America.

———. 2000b. *Employment-Based Health Insurance Coverage.* Washington, DC: Health Insurance Association of America.

Cutler, David, and Jon Gruber. 1996. Does Public Insurance Crowd out Private Insurance? *Quarterly Journal of Economics* 111:391–430.

Cutler, David M., and Jonathan Gruber. 1996. The Effect of Medicaid Expansions on Public Insurance, Private Insurance, and Redistribution. *The American Economic Review* 86(2):378–383.

Cutler, David M., and Jonathan Gruber. 1997. Medicaid and Private Insurance: Evidence and Implications. *Health Affairs* 16(1):194–200.

Davidoff, Amy J., A.B. Garrett, Diane J. Makuc, and Matthew Schirmer. 2000. Medicaid-Eligible Children Who Don't Enroll: Health Status, Access to Care, and Implications for Medicaid Enrollment. *Inquiry* 37:203–218.

Donelan, Karen, Catherine M. DesRoches, and Cathy Schoen. 2000. Inadequate Health Insurance: Costs and Consequences. *Medscape GeneralMed* 2(4):1–11.

Dubay, Lisa. 1999. *Expansions in Public Health Insurance and Crowd-Out: What the Evidence Says.* Washington, DC: The Henry J. Kaiser Family Foundation, The Kaiser Project On Incremental Health Reform. Accessed July 2, 2001. Available at http://www.kff.org/.

Dubay, Lisa and Genevieve Kenney. 1996. The Effects of Medicaid Expansions on Insurance Coverage of Children. *Future of Children* 6(1):152–161.

———. 1997. Did Medicaid Expansions for Pregnant Women Crowd Out Private Coverage? *Health Affairs* 16(1):185–193.

———. 2001. Health Care Access and Use Among Low-Income Children: Who Fares Best? *Health Affairs* 20(1):112–121.

Duncan, R. Paul, Karen Seccomebe, and Cheryl Amey. 1995. Changes in Health Insurance Coverage Within Rural and Urban Environments—1997 to 1997. *Journal of Rural Health* 11(3):169–176.

EBRI (Employee Benefit Research Institute). 2000. Employment-Based Health Care Benefits and Self-Funded Employment-Based Plans: An Overview. *Fact Sheet*. Washington, DC: Employee Benefit Research Institute.

———2001. EBRI Research Highlights: Health Data. Washington, DC: Employee Benefit Research Institute.

Eden, Jill. 1998. Measuring Access to Care Through Population-Based Surveys: Where Are We Now? *Health Services Research* 33(3):685–707.

Eisenberg, John M., and Elaine J. Power. 2000. Transforming Insurance Coverage Into Quality Health Care. *Journal of the American Medical Association* 284(16):2100–2107.

Farber, Henry, and Helen Levy. 2000. Recent Trends in Employer-Sponsored Health Insurance Coverage: Are Bad Jobs Getting Worse? *Journal of Health Economics* 19:93–119.

Foreman, J. 1992. Physicians Provide $6.8 Billion in Charity Care. *Archives of Ophthalmology* 110(9):1211.

Fronstin, Paul. 1998. Sources of Health Insurance and Characteristics of the Uninsured: Analysis of the March 1998 Current Population Survey. *Issue Brief No. 204*. Washington, DC: Employee Benefit Research Institute.

———. 1999. Employment-Based Health Insurance for Children: Why Did Coverage Increase in the Mid-1990s? *Health Affairs* 18(5):131–136.

———. 2000a. Counting the Uninsured: A Comparison of National Surveys. *Issue Brief No. 225*. Washington, DC: Employee Benefit Research Institute.

———. 2000b. *The Economic Costs of the Uninsured: Implications for Business and Government*. Washington, DC: Employee Benefit Research Institute.

———. 2000c. Job-Based Health Benefits Continue to Rise While Uninsured Rate Declines. *EBRI Notes* 21(11):1–8.

———. 2000d. Sources of Health Insurance and Characteristics of the Uninsured: Analysis of the March 2000 Current Population Survey. *Issue Brief No. 228*. Washington, DC: Employee Benefit Research Institute.

———. 2001. Employment-Based Health Benefits: Trends and Outlook. *Issue Brief No. 233*. Washington, DC: Employment Benefit Research Institute.

Fronstin, Paul, and Ruth Helman. 2000. Small Employers and Health Benefits: Findings from the 2000 Small Employer Health Benefits Survey. *Issue Brief No. 226*, and *Special Report SR35*. Washington DC: Employee Benefit Research Institute.

Fronstin, Paul, Lawrence G. Goldberg, and Philip K. Robins. 1997. Differences in Private Health Insurance Coverage for Working Male Hispanics. *Inquiry* 34:171–180.

Fronstin, Paul, and Sarah C. Snider. 1996-1997. An Examination of the Decline in Employment-Based Health Insurance Between 1988-1993. *Inquiry* 33(4):317–325.

Gabel, Jon. 1999. Job-Based Health Insurance, 1977–1998: The Accidental System Under Scrutiny. *Health Affairs* 18(6):62–74.

Gabel, Jon, Roger Formisano, Barbara Lohr, and Steven DiCarlo. 1991. Tracing the Cycle of Health Insurance. *Health Affairs* 11(4):48–61.

Gabel, Jon, Kelly Hunt, and Jean Kim. 1998. *The Financial Burden of Self-Paid Health Insurance on the Poor and Near Poor*. New York: The Commonwealth Fund.

Gabel, Jon, Kimberly Hurst, Heidi Whitmore, and Catherine Hoffman. 1999. Class and Benefits at the Workplace. *Health Affairs* 18(3):144–150.

Gabel, Jon, Larry Levitt, Jeremy Pickreign, Heidi Whitmore, et al. 2000. Job-Based Health Insurance in 2000: Premiums Rise Sharply While Coverage Grows. *Health Affairs* 19(5):144–151.

Gabel, Jon R., Paul G. Ginsburg, Jeremy D. Pickreign, and James D. Reschovsky. 2001. Trends In Out-Of-Pocket Spending By Insured American Workers, 1990–1997. *Health Affairs* 20(2):47–57.

Garrett, Bowen, and John Holahan. 2000. Health Insurance Coverage After Welfare. *Health Affairs* 19(1):175–184.

Gaskin, Darrell J. 1999. *Safety Net Hospitals: Essential Providers of Public Health and Specialty Services.* New York: The Commonwealth Fund.

Glied, Sherry, and Mark Stabile. 2001. Generation Vexed: Age-Cohort Differences in Employer-Sponsored Health Insurance Coverage. *Health Affairs* 20(1):184-91.

Grumbach, Kevin, Dennis Keane, and Andrew Bindman. 1993. Primary Care and Public Emergency Department Overcrowding. *American Journal of Public Health* 83(3):372–378.

Guendelman, Sylvia, Helen Halpin Schauffler, and Michelle Pearl. 2001. Unfriendly Shores: How Immigrant Children Fare in the U.S Health System. *Health Affairs* 20(1):257–266.

Guyer, Jocelyn, and Cindy Mann. 1999. *Employed But Not Insured. A State-by-State Analysis of the Number of Low-Income Working Parents Who Lack Health Insurance.* Washington, DC: Center on Budget and Policy Priorities. Accessed May 20, 2001. Available at http://www.cbpp.org

Guyer, Jocelyn. 2000. Health Care After Welfare: An Update of Findings from State-Level Leaver Studies. Washington, DC: Center on Budget and Policy Priorities. Accessed May 7, 2001. Available at http://www.cbpp.org.

Guyer, Jocelyn, Matthew Broaddus, and Annie Dude. 2001. *Millions of Mothers Lack Health Insurance Coverage.* Washington, DC: Center on Budget and Policy Priorities. Accessed May 10, 2001. Available at http://www.cbpp.org

Hadley, Jack, Earl P. Steinberg, and Judith Feder. 1991. Comparison of Uninsured and Privately Insured Hosptal Patients. *Journal of the American Medical Association* 265(3):374–379.

Hafner-Eaton, Chris. 1993. Physician Utilization Disparities Between the Uninsured and Insured. Comparisons of the Chronically Ill, Acutely Ill, and Well Nonelderly Populations. *Journal of the American Medical Association* 269(6):787–792.

Haley, Jennifer M., and Stephen Zuckerman. 2000. *Health Insurance, Access, and Use: United States. Tabulations from the 1997 National Survey of America's Families.* Washington, DC: The Urban Institute.

Hall, Mark A. 2000. The Structure and Enforcement of Health Insurance Rating Reforms. *Inquiry* 37(4):376-388.

Hanson, Karla L. 1998. Is Insurance for Children Enough? The Link Between Parents' and Children's Health Care Use Revisited. *Inquiry* 35(3):294–302.

———. 2001. Patterns of Insurance Coverage Within Families With Children. *Health Affairs* 20(1):240–246.

Hartley, David, Lois Quam, and Nicole Lurie. 1994. Urban and Rural Differences in Health Insurance and Access to Care. *Journal of Rural Health* 10(2):98–108.

HCFA (Health Care Financing Administration). 2000a. *HIPAA Online.* Accessed July 16, 2001. Available at http://www.hcfa.gov/Medicaid/hipaa/online/default.asp.

———. 2000b. *Medicare Enrollment Trends 1966–1999.* Accessed May 4, 2001. Available at http://www.hcfa.gov/stats/anrltend.htm.

———. 2001. *Medicaid Beneficiaries, Vendor, Medical Assistance and Administrative Assistance.* Accessed March 26, 2001. Available at http://www.hcfa.gov/medicaid/msis/2082-1.htm.

Heffler, Stephen, Katherine Levit, Sheila Smith, Cynthia Smith, et al. 2001. Health Spending Growth Up in 1999. Faster Growth Expected in the Future. *Health Affairs* 20(2):193–213.

Himmelstein, David U., and Steffie Woolhandler. 1995. Care Denied: U.S. Residents Who Are Unable to Obtain Needed Medical Services. *American Journal of Public Health* 85(3): 341–344.

Hoffman, Catherine, and Mary Pohl. 2000. *Health Insurance Coverage in America: 1999 Data Update.* Washington, DC: The Kaiser Commission on Medicaid and the Uninsured.

Hoffman, Catherine, and Alan Schlobohm. 2000. *Uninsured in America: A Chart Book.* Washington, DC: The Henry J. Kaiser Family Foundation.

Hoffman, Catherine, Dorothy P. Rice, and Hai-Yen Sung. 1996. Persons with Chronic Conditions, their Prevalence and Costs. *Journal of the American Medical Association.* 276(18):1473–1479.

Holahan, John. 2001. *Why Did the Number of Uninsured Fall in 1999?* Washington, DC: The Kaiser Commission on Medicaid and the Uninsured.

Holahan, John, Leighton Ku, and Mary Pohl. 2001. *Is Immigration Responsible for the Growth in the Number of Uninsured?* Issue Paper 2221. Washington, DC: The Kaiser Commission on Medicaid and the Uninsured.

Holahan, John, and Niall Brennan. 2000. *Who Are the Adult Uninsured?* Series B, B-14. Washington, DC: The Urban Institute.

Holahan, John, and Johnny Kim. 2000. Why Does the Number of Uninsured Americans Continue to Grow? *Health Affairs* 19(4):188–196.

Holahan, John, Colin Winterbottom, and Shruti Rajan. 1995. A Shifting Picture of Health Insurance Coverage. *Health Affairs* 14(4):253–264.

Hsia, Judith, Elizabeth Kemper, Shoshanna Sofaer, Deborah Bowen, et al. 2000. Is Insurance a More Important Determinant of Healthcare Access Than Perceived Health? Evidence from the Women's Health Initiative. *Journal of Women's Health & Gender-Based Medicine* 9(8):881–889.

Huang, Fung-Yea. 1997. Health Insurance Coverage of the Children of Immigrants in the United States. *Maternal Child Health Journal* 1(2):69–80.

IOM (Institute of Medicine). 1990. *Medicine: A Strategy for Quality Assurance.* Washington, DC: National Academy Press.

———. 1993. *Employment and Health Benefits.* Washington, DC: National Academy Press.

———. 1996. *Primary Care: America's Health in a New Era.* Washington, DC: National Academy Press.

———. 2000. *America's Health Care Safety Net: Intact but Endangered.* Washington, DC: National Academy Press.

———. 2001. *Crossing the Quality Chasm: A Health System for the 21st Century.* Washington, DC: National Academy Press.

Jensen, Gail A. 1992. The Dynamics of Health Insurance Among the Near Elderly. *Medical Care* 30(7):598–614.

Kaiser Commission on Medicaid and the Uninsured. 2001. *The Uninsured and Their Access to Health Care.* Fact Sheet. Washington, DC: The Kaiser Commission on Medicaid and the Uninsured.

Kaiser Family Foundation–Health Research and Educational Trust (HRET). 2000. *Employer Health Benefits, 2000. Annual Survey.* Washington, DC: The Henry J. Kaiser Family Foundation.

Kasper, Judith D. 1998. Asking About Access: Challenges for Surveys in a Changing Healthcare Environment. *Health Services Research* 33(3):715-39.

Kasper, Judith D., Terence A. Giovannini, and Catherine Hoffman. 2000. Gaining and Losing Health Insurance: Strengthening the Evidence for Effects of Access to Care and Health Outcomes. *Medical Care Research and Review* 57(3): 298–318.

Kenney, Genevieve, and Jennifer Haley. 2001. *Why Aren't More Uninsured Children Enrolled in Medicaid or SCHIP?* Series B, No.B-35. Washington, DC: The Urban Institute, Assessing the New Federalism, National Survey of America's Families. Accessed July 6, 2001. Available at http://newfederalism.urban.org/.

Kenney, Genevieve, Stephen Zuckerman, Shruti Rajan, Niall Brennan, et al. 1999. The National Survey of America's Families: An Overview of the Health Policy Component. *Inquiry* 36:353–362.

Kenney, Genevieve, Jennifer Haley, and Lisa Dubay. 2001. *How Familiar Are Low-Income Parents with Medicaid and SCHIP?* Series B, No.B-34. Washington, DC: The Urban Institute, Assessing the New Federalism. Accessed July 6, 2001. Available at http://newfederalism.urban.org/.

Klein, Rachel. 2000. *Go Directly to Work, Do Not Collect Health Insurance: Low-Income Parents Lose Medicaid.* Washington, DC: Families USA. Accessed May 20, 2001. Available at http://www.familiesusa.org.

Kolata, Gina. 2001. Medical Fees Are Often Higher for Patients Without Insurance. *The New York Times.* Accessed July 9, 2001. Available at http://www.nytimes.com.2001/04/02/National/02insu.html.

Kozak, Lola Jean, Margaret J. Hall, and Maria F. Owings. 2001. Trends in Avoidable Hospitalizations, 1980–1998. *Health Affairs* 20(2):225–232.

Kronebusch, Karl. 2001. Medicaid for Children: Federal Mandates, Welfare Reform, and Policy Backsliding. *Health Affairs* 20(1):97–111.

Kronick, Richard, and Todd Gilmer. 1999. Explaining the Decline in Health Insurance Coverage. *Health Affairs* 18(2):1–17.

Ku, Leighton and Shannon Blaney. 2000. *Health Coverage for Legal Immigrant Children: New Census Data Highlight Importance of Restoring Medicaid and SCHIP Coverage*. Washington, DC: Center on Budget and Policy Priorities. Accessed January 10, 2001. Available at http://www.cbpp.org.

Ku, Leighton, and Sheetal Matani. 2001. Left Out: Immigrants' Access to Health Care and Insurance. *Health Affairs* 20(1):247–256.

Lave, Judith R., Christopher R. Keane, J. Lin Chyongchiou, et al. 1998. The Impact of Lack of Health Insurance on Children. *Journal of Health Social Policy* 10(2):57–73.

Levit, Katherine R., G. L. Olin, and Suzanne W. Letsch. 1992. Americans' Health Insurance Coverage, 1980–91. *Health Care Financing Review* 14:31–57.

Lewis, Kimball, Marilyn Ellwood, and John L. Czajka. 1998. *Counting the Uninsured: A Review of the Literature*. Washington, DC: The Urban Institute.

Long, Stephen H., and M. Susan Marquis. 1999. Stability and Variation in Employment-Based Health Insurance Coverage. *Health Affairs* 18(6):133–139.

Long, Stephen H., and Jack Rodgers. 1995. Do Shifts Toward Service Industries, Part-Time Work, and Self-Employment Explain the Rising Uninsured Rate? *Inquiry* 32:111–116.

Lurie, Nicole, N.B. Ward, Martin F. Shapiro, and Robert H. Brook. 1984. Termination from Medi-Cal: Does It Affect Health? *New England Journal of Medicine* 311:480–484.

Lurie, Nicole, N.B. Ward, Martin F. Shapiro, et al. 1986. Termination of Medi-Cal Benefits: A Follow Up Study One Year Later. *New England Journal of Medicine* 314:1266–1268.

Lutzky, Amy Westpfahl, and Ian Hill. 2001. *Has the Jury Reached a Verdict? States' Early Experiences with Crowd Out under SCHIP*. Occasional Paper No. 47. Washington, DC: The Urban Institute. Accessed July 6, 2001. Available at http://newfederalism.urban.org/.

Mann, Joyce. M., Glenn A. Melnick, Anil Bamezai, and Jack Zwanziger. 1997. A Profile of Uncompensated Hospital Care, 1983–1995. *Health Affairs* 16(4):223–232.

Marmor, Theodore R., and Morris L. Barer. 1995. Health Care Reform in the United States: On the Road to Nowhere Again? *Social Science and Medicine* 41(4):453–460.

Marquis, M. Susan and Stephen H. Long. 1994–1995. The Uninsured Access Gap: Narrowing the Estimates. *Inquiry* 31(4):405–414.

———. 1995. Worker Demand for Health Insurance in the Non-Group Market. *Journal of Health Economics* 14(1): 47–63.

———. 1999. Recent Trends in Self-Insured Employer Health Plans. *Health Affairs* 18(3): 161–166.

Marsteller, Jill A., Len M. Nichols, Adam Badawi, Bethany Kessler, et al. 1998. *Variations in the Uninsured: State and County Level Analyses*. Washington, DC: Urban Institute. Accessed May 1, 2001. Available at www.ui.org/.

McArdle, Frank, Steve Coppock, Dale Yamamoto, and Andrew Zebrak. 1999. *Retiree Health Coverage: Recent Trends and Employer Perspectives on Future Benefits*. Washington, DC: The Henry J. Kaiser Family Foundation.

McBride, Timothy D. 1997. Uninsured Spells of the Poor. Prevalence and Duration. *Health Care Financing Review* 19(1): 145–160.

McDonnell, Kenneth J., and Paul Fronstin. 1999. *EBRI Health Benefits Databook*. Washington, DC: Employee Benefit Research Institute.

Medoff, James L., Howard B. Shapiro, Michael Calabrese, and Andrew D. Harless. 2001. *How The New Labor Market Is Squeezing Workforce Health Benefits*. Publication No. 449. New York, NY: The Commonwealth Fund. Accessed June 20, 2001. Available at http://www.cmwf.org/.

Miles, Steven, and Kara Parker. 1997. Men, Women and Health Insurance. *New England Journal of Medicine* 336(3): 218–221.

Mills, Robert J. 2000. Health Insurance Coverage, 1999. *Current Population Reports.* P 60-211. Washington, DC: U.S. Census Bureau.

Millman, Michael (ed). 1993. *Access to Health Care in America.* Washington, DC: National Academy Press.

Monheit, Alan C., M. M. Hogan, M. L. Berk, et al. 1985. The Employed Uninsured and the Role of Public Policy. *Inquiry* 22:348–364.

Monheit, Alan C., Barbara S. Schone, and Amy K. Taylor. 1999. Health Insurance Choices in Two-Worker Households: Determinants of Double Coverage. *Inquiry* 36:12–29.

Monheit, Alan C., and Jessica Primoff Vistnes. 2000. Race/Ethnicity and Health Insurance Status: 1987 and 1996. *Medical Care Research Review* 57 (Suppl.) 1:11–35.

Monheit, Alan C., Jessica P. Vistnes, and John M. Eisenberg. 2001. Moving to Medicare: Trends in the Health Insurance Status of Near-Elderly Workers, 1987–1996. *Health Affairs* 20(2):204–213.

Morrisey, Michael A. 1993. Mandated Benefits and Compensating Differentials: Taxing the Uninsured. In: Robert Helms (ed.) *American Health Policy: Critical Issues for Reform.* Washington, DC: American Enterprise Institute. Pp. 133–157.

Mueller, Keith, Patil Kashinath, and Eugene Boilesen. 1998. The Role of Uninsurance and Race in Healthcare Utilization by Rural Minorities. *Health Services Research* 33(3):597–610.

Mueller, Keith J., Kashinath Patil, and Fred Ullrich. 1997. Lengthening Spells of Uninsurance and Their Consequences. *Journal of Rural Health* 13(1):29–37.

Mutual of Omaha. 2000. Web page. Accessed May 11, 2001. Available at www.mutualofomaha.com/acrodoc/group/mug6440.pdf.

Newacheck, Paul W., Jeffery J. Stoddard, and Dana C. Hughes. 1998. Health Insurance and Access to Primary Care for Children. *New England Journal of Medicine* 338(8):513–518.

Newhouse, Joseph P., and the Insurance Experiment Group. 1993. *Free For All? Lessons from the RAND Health Insurance Experiment.* Cambridge, MA: Harvard University Press.

NewsHour with Jim Lehrer/Kaiser Family Foundation. 2000. National Survey on the Uninsured. Menlo Park, CA: The Henry J. Kaiser Family Foundation.

Nichols, Len M. 2000. State Regulation. What Have We Learned So Far? *Journal of Health Policy, Politics, and Law* 25(1):175–196.

Nichols, Len M., and Linda J. Blumberg. 1998. A Different Kind of "New Federalism"? The Health Insurance Portability and Accountablity Act of 1996. *Health Affairs* 17(3):25-42.

Numbers, Ronald L. 1985. The Third Party: Health Insurance in America. In: Judith Leavitt and Ronald Numbers (eds.), *Sickness and Health in America. Readings in the History of Medicine and Public Health.* Madison, WI: University of Wisconsin Press. Pp. 233–247.

O'Brien, Patrick M., Kimberly A. Collins, Thomas D. Kirsch, Daniel A. Pollock, et al. 1999. The Emergency Department as a Public Safety Net. *Defending America's Safety Net.* Dallas, TX: American College of Emergency Physicians.

O'Brien, Ellen, and Judith Feder. 1999. *Employment-Based Health Insurance Coverage and Its Decline: The Growing Plight of Low-Wage Workers.* Washington, DC: The Kaiser Commission on Medicaid and the Uninsured.

O'Brien, Ellen and Judith Feder. 1998. *How Well Does the Employment-Based Health Insurance System Work for Low-Income Families?* Issue Paper. Washington, DC: The Kaiser Commission on Medicaid and the Uninsured.

Ormond, Barbara A., Stephen Zuckerman, and Aparna Lhila. 2001. Rural/Urban Differences in Health Care Are Not Uniform Across States, Series B, B-11. Washington, DC: The Urban Institute. Accessed March 26, 2001. Available at http://newfederalism.urban.org.

Pauly, Mark V., and Allison M. Percy. 2000. Cost and Performance: A Comparison of the Individual and Group Health Insurance Markets. *Journal of Health Politics, Policy and Law* 25(1):9–26.

Pane, Gregg, Michael C. Farner, and Kym A. Salness. 1991. Health Care Access Problems of Medically Indigent Emergency Department Walk-In Patients. *Annals of Emergency Medicine* 20(7):730–733.

Pauly, Mark, and Bradley Herring. 1999. *Pooling Health Insurance Risk*. Washington, DC: American Enterprise Institute Press.

Perry, Michael, Susan Kannel, R. Burciaga Valdez, and Christina Chang. 2000. *Medicaid and Children: Overcoming Barriers to Enrollment, Findings from a National Survey*. Washington, DC: Kaiser Commission on Medicaid and the Uninsured.

Pol, Louis. 2000. Health Insurance in Rural America. *Rural Policy Brief* 5(11).

Pollitz, Karen, Richard Sorian, and Kathy Thomas. 2001. *How Accessible is Individual Health Insurance for Consumers in Less-Than-Perfect Health?* Publication No. 3133. Washington, DC: The Henry J. Kaiser Family Foundation. Accessed June 20, 2001. Available at http://www.kff.org/.

Porter Novelli. 2001. *Focus Group Research on Perceptions that Currently Frame the Issue of the Uninsured in America*. Unpublished study conducted for The Robert Wood Johnson Foundation, Washington, DC.

Quinn, Kevin. 2000. *Working Without Benefits: The Health Insurance Crisis Confronting Hispanic Americans*. Pub. No. 370. New York: The Commonwealth Fund, Task Force on the Future of Health Insurance for Working Americans.

Quinn, Kevin, Cathy Schoen, and Louisa Buatti. 2000. *On Their Own: Young Adults Living Without Health Insurance*. Pub. No. 391. New York: The Commonwealth Fund, Task Force on the Future of Health Insurance for Working Americans.

Rhoades, Jeffrey and M. Chu. 2000. *Health Insurance Status of Civilian Noninstitutionalized Population*. MEPS Research Findings. 01-0011. Rockville, MD: Agency for Healthcare Research and Quality.

Rhoades, Jeffrey, E. Richard Brown, and Jessica Primoff Vistnes. 2000. *Health Insurance Status of the Civilian Noninstitutionalized Population: 1998*. AHRQ Pub. No. 00-0023. Rockville, MD: Agency for Healthcare Research and Quality.

Ricketts, Thomas C. III, Karen D. Johnson-Webb, and Randy K. Randolph. 1999. Populations and Places in Rural America. In: Thomas C. Ricketts III (ed.) *Rural Health in the United States*. New York: Oxford University Press. Pp. 7–24.

Riley, Trish. 1999. How Will We Know if CHIP Is Working? *Health Affairs* 18(2):64–66.

Rosenbaum, Sara. 2000. Medicaid Eligibility and Citizenship Status: Policy Implications for Immigrant Populations. Policy Brief no. 2201. Washington, DC: Kaiser Commission on Medicaid and the Uninsured. Accessed May 7, 2001. Available at http://www.kff.org.

Rowland, Diane, Judith Feder, and Patricia Seliger Keenan. 1998. Uninsured in America: The Causes and Consequences. In: Stuart H. Altman, Reinhart Uwe E., and Alexandra E. Shields (eds.) *The Future U.S. Healthcare System: Who Will Care for the Poor and Uninsured?* Chicago, IL: Health Administration Press. Pp. 25–44.

Salisbury, Dallas. 2001. *EBRI Research Highlights: Retirement and Health Data*. Washington DC: Employee Benefit Research Institute.

Saver, Barry G., and Mark P. Doescher. 1999. To Buy, or Not to Buy. Factors Associated With Purchase of Nongroup, Private Health Insurance. *Medical Care* 38(2):141–151.

Schoen, Cathy, and Catherine DesRoches. 2000. Uninsured and Unstably Insured: The Importance of Continuous Insurance Coverage. *Health Services Research* 35(1):187–206.

Schoen, Cathy, and Elaine Puleo. 1998. Low-Income Working Families at Risk: Uninsured and Underserved. *Journal of Urban Health* 75(1):30–49.

Schur, Claudia L., Marc L. Berk, Cynthia D. Good, and Eric N. Gardner. 1999. *California's Undocumented Latino Immigrants: A Report on Access to Health Care Services*. Washington, DC: The Henry J. Kaiser Family Foundation.

Schur, Claudia L., and Jacob Feldman. 2001. *Running In Place: How Job Characteristics, Immigrant Status, and Family Structure Keep Hispanics Uninsured*. Publication No. 453. New York, NY: The Commonwealth Fund. Accessed June 20, 2001. Available at http://www.cmwf.org/.

Schur, Claudia L., and Sheila J. Franco. 1999. Access to Health Care. In: Thomas C. Ricketts III (ed.) *Rural Health in the United States*. New York: Oxford University Press. Pp. 25–37.

Selden, Thomas M., Jessica S. Banthin, and Joel W. Cohen. 1999. Waiting in the Wings: Eligibility and Enrollment in the State Children's Health Insurance Program. *Health Affairs* 18(2):126–133.

Sheils, John, and Paul Hogan. 1999. Cost of Tax-Exempt Health Benefits in 1998. *Health Affairs* 18(2):176–181.

Sheils, John, Paul Hogan, and Randall Haught. 1999. *Health Insurance and Taxes: The Impact of Proposed Changes in Current Federal Policy*. Washington, DC: The National Coalition on Health Care.

Shi, Leiyu. 2000a. Type of Health Insurance and Quality of Primary Care Experience. *American Journal of Public Health* 90(12):1848–1855.

———. 2000b. Vulnerable Populations and Health Insurance. *Medical Care Research and Review* 57(1):110–134.

Short, Pamela F. 1998. Gaps and Transitions in Health Insurance: What Are the Concerns of Women? *Journal of Women's Health* 7(6):725–737.

Short, Pamela F. and Vicki A. Freedman. 1998. Single Women and the Dynamics of Medicaid. *Health Services Research* 33(5):1309–1336.

Short, Pamela Farley, and Jacob Alex Klerman. 1998. *Targeting Long- and Short-Term Gaps in Health Insurance*. New York, NY: The Commonwealth Fund. Accessed July 3, 2001. Available at http://www.cmwf.org/programs/insurance/.

Short, Pamela F., Beth A. Hahn, Karen Beauregard, P. Holly Harvey, et al. 1997. The Effect of Universal Coverage on Health Expenditures for the Uninsured. *Medical Care* 35(2):95–113.

Sox, Colin M., Katherine Swartz, Helen R. Burstin, and Troyen A. Brennan. 1998. Insurance or a Regular Physician: Which is the Most Powerful Predictor of Health Care. *American Journal of Public Health* 88(3):364–370.

Spillman, Brenda C. 2000. Adults Without Health Insurance: Do State Policies Matter? *Health Affairs* 19(4):178–187.

Starfield, Barbara. 1995. Access—Perceived or Real, and to What? *Journal of the American Medical Association* 274(4):346–347.

Starr, Paul. 1982. *The Social Transformation of American Medicine*. New York: Basic Books.

Stevens, Rosemary. 1989. *In Sickness and In Wealth: America's Hospitals in the Twentieth Century*. New York: Basic Books.

Stone, Deborah. 1993. The Struggle for the Soul of Health Insurance. *Journal of Health Politics, Policy and Law* 18(2):287–317.

Swartz, Katherine. 2001. *Rising Health Care Costs and Numbers of People Without Health Insurance*. Unpublished manuscript, presented at the Council on the Economic Impact of Health System Change. Washington, DC.

———. 2000. *Markets for Individual Health Insurance: Can We Make Them Work with Incentives to Purchase Insurance?* New York, NY: The Commonwealth Fund. Accessed January 24, 2001. Available at http://www.cmwf.org/.

———. 1998. All Uninsured Are Not the Same. In: Stuart H. Altman, Reinhart Uwe E., and Alexandra E. Shields (eds.) *The Future of the U.S. Healthcare System: Who Will Care for the Uninsured*. Chicago, IL: Health Administration Press. Pp. 45–66.

———. 1997. Changes in the 1995 Current Population Survey and Estimates of Health Insurance Coverage. *Inquiry* 34(1):70–79.

———. 1996. Medicaid Crowd Out and the Inverse Truman Bind. *Inquiry* 33(1):5–8.

———. 1986. Interpreting the Estimates from Four National Surveys of the Number of People without Health Insurance. *Journal of Economic and Social Measurement* 14(3):233-43.

Swartz, Katherine, and Timothy D. McBride. 1990. Spells Without Health Insurance: Distributions of Durations and Their Link to Point-in-Time Estimates of the Uninsured. *Inquiry* 27(3):281–288.

Swartz, Katherine, John Marcotte, and Timothy D. McBride. 1993a. Personal Characteristics and Spells Without Health Insurance. *Inquiry* 30(1):64–76.

————. 1993b. Spells Without Health Insurance: The Distribution of Durations When Left-Censored Spells Are Included. *Inquiry* 30(1):77–83.

Thorpe, Kenneth, and Curtis S. Florence. 1999. Why Are Workers Uninsured? Employer-Sponsored Health Insurance in 1997. *Health Affairs* 18(2):213–218.

Thorpe, Kenneth E., and Curtis S. Florence. 1998. *Covering Uninsured Children and Their Parents: Estimated Costs and Number of Newly Insured.* New York, NY: The Commonwealth Fund.

U.S. Census Bureau. 2000. Current Population Reports. *Money Income in the United States: 1999.* P60-209. Washington, DC: U.S. Government Printing Office. Accessed April 17, 2001. Available at http://www.census.gov

————. 2001. Ranking Table for States: 1990 and 2000. Accessed May 3, 2001. Available at http://www.census.gov/population/cen2000/phc-t2/tab01.pdf.

U.S. Department of Commerce. 1975. *Historical Statistics of the United States, Colonial Times to 1970.* Washington, DC: U.S. Government Printing Office.

U.S. Department of Health and Human Services. Office of the Assistant Secretary for Planning and Evaluation. 1999. *The 1999 HHS Poverty Guidelines.* Accessed January 24, 2001. Available at http://aspe.hhs.gov/poverty/99poverty.htm.

U.S. Department of Health and Human Services. Office of the Assistant Secretary for Planning and Evaluation. 2000. *The 2000 HHS Poverty Guidelines.* Accessed January 24, 2001. Available at http://aspe.hhs.gov/poverty/00poverty.htm.

U.S. Department of Labor. 2001. Mass Layoffs in April 2001. *Bureau of Labor Statistics News* USDL 01-156. Washington, DC: Bureau of Labor Statistics.

U.S. GAO (U.S. General Accounting Office). 1996. *Private Health Insurance: Millions Relying on Individual Market Face Cost and Coverage Trade-Offs.* Washington, DC: U.S. Government Printing Office.

————. 1997a. *Employment-Based Health Insurance: Cost Increases and Family Coverage Decreases.* GAO/HEHS-97-35. Washington, DC: U.S. Government Printing Office.

————. 1997b. *Private Health Insurance: Continued Erosion of Coverage Linked to Cost Pressures.* GAO/HEHS-97-122. Washington, DC: U.S. Government Printing Office.

————. 1998. *Private Health Insurance. Declining Employer Coverage May Affect Access for 55- to 64- Year-Olds.* GAO/HEHE-98-133. Washington, DC: U.S. Government Printing Office.

————. 2001a. *Health Insurance: Characteristics and Trends in the Uninsured Population.* GAO, GAO-01-507T. Washington, DC: U.S. Government Printing Office.

————. 2001b. *Retiree Health Benefits,* GAO-01-374, Washington, DC: U.S. Government Printing Office.

U.S. Immigration and Naturalization Service (INS). 2001. *Illegal Alien Resident Population.* Accessed July 17, 2001. Available at http://www.ins.gov/graphics/aboutins/statistics/illegalalien/index.html.

U.S. Office of Personnel Management. 2000. *The 2001 Guide to Federal Employees Health Benefits Plans.* RI 70-1. Washington, DC: U.S. Government Printing Office.

Valdez, R. Burciaga, Hal Morgenstern, E. Richard Brown, et al. 1993. Insuring Latinos Against the Costs of Illness. *Journal of the American Medical Association* 269(7): 889–894.

Weinick, Robin M., Samuel H. Zuvekas, and Susan K. Drilea. 1997. Access to Health Care—Sources and Barriers: 1996. *MEPS Research Findings No. 3.* AHCPR Pub. No. 98-0001. Rockville, MD: Agency for Health Care Policy and Research.

Weinick, Robin M., and Alan C. Monheit. 1999. Children's Health Insurance Coverage and Family Structure, 1977–1996. *Medical Care Research and Review* 56(1):55–73.

Weinick, Robin M., Samuel H. Zuvekas, and Joel W. Cohen. 2000. Racial and Ethnic Differences in Access to and Use of Health Care Services, 1977 to 1996. *Medical Care Research Review* 57 (Suppl.). 1:36–54.

Weissman, Joel. S., and Arnold M. Epstein. 1994. *Falling Through the Safety Net: Insurance Status and Access to Health Care.* Baltimore, MD: Johns Hopkins University Press.

Weissman, Joel S., Constantine Gatsonis, and Arnold M. Epstein. 1992. Rates of Avoidable Hospitalization by Insurance Status in Massachusetts and Maryland. *Journal of the American Medical Association* 268(17):2388–2394.

Wielawski, Irene. 2000. Gouging the Medically Uninsured: A Tale of Two Bills. *Health Affairs* 19(5):180–185.

Wirthlin Worldwide. 2001. *Uninsured Phone Study: January 12–23, 2001.* Unpublished survey conducted for The Robert Wood Johnson Foundation. McLean, VA.

Wolfe, Barbara L. 1994. Reform of Health Care for the Nonelderly Poor. In: Sheldon Sandefur, Gary D. Danziger, and Daniel H. Weinberg (eds.) *Confronting Poverty Prescriptions for Change.* Cambridge, MA: Harvard University Press. Pp. 253–288.

Wolman, Dianne. 1992. High-Risk Pools. In: John Goddeeris, and Andrew Hogan (eds.) *Improving Access to Health Care.* Kalamazoo, MI: W.E. Upjohn Institute for Employment Research. Pp. 123–137.

Wyn, Roberta, Beatriz Solis, Victoria Ojeda, and Nadereh Pourat. 2001. *Falling Through the Cracks: Health Insurance Coverage of Low-Income Women.* Los Angeles, CA: UCLA Center for Health Policy Research.

Yazici, Esel Y., and Robert Kaestner. 2000. Medicaid Expansions and the Crowding Out of Private Health Insurance Among Children. *Inquiry* 37(1):23–32.

Zimmerman, D.R., K.A. MacCarten-Gibbs, D.J. DeNoble, C. Bojrgo, et al. 1996. Repeat Pediatrics Visits to a General Emergency Department. *Annals of Emergency Medicine* 28(5):467–473.

Zuckerman, Stephen, Genevieve M. Kenney, Lisa Dubay, Jennifer Haley, et al. 2001. Shifting Health Insurance Coverage, 1997-1999. *Health Affairs* 20(1):169–177.

Zuvekas, Samuel H., and Robin M. Weinick. 1999. Changes in Access to Care, 1977–1996: The Role of Health Insurance. *Health Services Research* 34(1):271–279.

Zweifel, P. J., and Willard G. Manning. 2000. Consumer Incentives in Health Care. In: Anthony J. Culyer and Joseph P. Newhouse (eds.) *Handbook of Health Economics.* Amsterdam: Elsevier. Pp. 410–459.